CRAFTWAYS

CRAFTWAYS

On the Organization of Scholarly Work

Second Enlarged Edition

Aaron Wildavsky

Transaction Publishers

New Brunswick (U.S.A.) and London (U.K.)

Third printing 2004

Copyright © 1993 by Aaron Wildavsky. Published by Transaction Publishers, New Brunswick, New Jersey. Previous edition copyright © 1989.

Library of Congress Catalog Number: 92-44532
ISBN: 1-56000-696-X
Printed in the United States of America

Library of Congress Cataloging-in-Publication Data

Wildavsky, Aaron B.
  Craftways : on the organization of scholarly work / Aaron Wildavsky.—
2nd ed.
        p. cm.
  Includes bibliographical references and index.
  ISBN 1-56000-696-X (pbk.)
  1. Learning and scholarship. 2. Research—Methodology. 3. Scholarly
publishing. 4. Authorship. I. Title.

AZ105.W48 1993
808' .02—dc20   92-44532
                                                               CIP

To my friend and father-in-law,
Edward Cadman,
a superlative craftsman

Contents

ACKNOWLEDGMENTS

Those who are interested in exploring craftways can do no better than read C. Wright Mills' exemplary "On Intellectual Craftsmanship" in *The Sociological Imagination* (New York: Oxford Press, 1959); Howard Becker's *Writing for Social Scientists* (Chicago: University of Chicago Press, 1986); or Richard Fenno's "Notes on Method: Participant Observation" in his *Home Style: House Members in Their Districts* (Boston: Little, Brown, 1978). When scholarly work gets too difficult and, above all, too serious, there is no better antidote than Robert K. Merton's marvelous *On the Shoulders of Giants, a Shandean Postscript* (New York: Harcourt, Brace, 1965).

Several colleagues have shared their comments on parts of the manuscript with me: Howard Becker, Lewis Dexter, Irving Horowitz, Ted Lascher, Gary Marx, and Selma Monsky. I appreciate their comments, especially when their views of craftsmanship differed from mine.

Preface to the Second Edition

My aim is to make this second edition an introduction to the norms and mores of political science in particular and social science in general. Majors in social science disciplines and graduate students seeking a professional identity are taught anything and everything but, arguably, what they most want to know: What kind of person is a political scientist or sociologist or psychologist or policy analyst? How do and how ought social scientists treat one another? What does excellence consist of in research and in teaching? Are these twin tasks inevitably opposed (the more research, the usual story goes, the less teaching) or may they be made compatible or even reinforcing? How should good social scientists behave?

Thus I have replaced those essays that are more personal with new ones that are more about the profession. The final section, "The Profession," contains four new essays and a book review. It begins with "Talking and Teaching," taking the would-be social scientist from her "job talk" to giving seminars and lectures with their special requirements. I argue that being an effective speaker should be part of professional pride. "On Being a Department Chair" is not only about the political administration of an academic department in a university during a troubled time; it is also about the norms, and conflict over norms, of academic life.

The last three pieces are about new challenges for the study of politics and society. In earlier times, to begin with, I did not think it necessary to read articles in scientific journals and now I think it is. As the environmental and safety movements grow stronger, so that questions of private behavior and public policy of great importance are raised with ever-greater frequency, researchers, faculty, as well as students, I believe, should train themselves to read the original science. Expectations for scholars and teachers, the professional point is, do (and should) change with the times.

Anyone who thinks he had it tough as a student need only consider the bewildering array of perspectives facing beginning social scientists today. From being told to be more scientific to being warned that science is a snare, from being told the scholar's obligation is to learn about his tradition to hearing that tradition is a form of oppression, from learning about the virtues of clarity to being told that each sentence negates whatever came before, social scientists face ever-greater uncertainty not only about how good an explanation they provide but about what sort of explanation is worth providing.

My view on objectivity is that it is worth striving toward not only for each scholar individually but even more for social science as a profession collectively. The concluding book review gives my position that incorporating new theories, like cultural analysis, and new methods, like social construction, is entirely compatible with the strictest standards of falsification and verification. What is the point, I ask, of trying out new theories and methods if one simultaneously rigs the rules in their favor?

Craftways: An Introduction to the Organization of Scholarly Work

*No human pursuit achieves dignity until it can be
called work, and . . . you . . . experience a
physical loneliness for the tools of your trade. . . .*
Beryl Markham,
West with the Night

Collected essays usually gather dust. While this is not the worst fate imaginable (compared, say, to allowing one's paper to languish in deserved obscurity), I have a different future in mind. My aim is to write volumes composed of essays on the subjects that have interested me most—political culture, the presidency, budgeting, federalism, foreign and defense policy, policy analysis, political parties—so as to say things of interest to contemporary readers. I want books that will stand on their own. Therefore I will include nothing that, in my opinion, has no lasting significance. Where articles have become dated, I will bring them up-to-date. Where there is more (or less) worth saying, I will try (not) to say it. Every volume will include new essays. Where the value of the work consists of the predictions it made, I will leave the piece unchanged, however badly the world has treated it, writing a postscript to explore the discrepancy. And should these volumes find favor, I will bring out revised editions, with corrections of old errors and commission of new ones, so as to keep faith with my conception of collected essays as a living and growing organism, not gray with dust but green with life.

It seems appropriate to begin this series with the scholarly craft itself. For as long as I can remember, I have been interested in craftsmanship, in the combination of the scholarly calling with better ways of doing things. As time went on, I could not help but notice from numerous queries ("How do you get so much done?") that others were interested in my work ways. This accounts for the combination of the personal and the prescriptive found here.

Acknowledgment of interest in how to work was responsible for the essays that began an earlier collection—*The Revolt against the Masses.*[1] The section of the introduction entitled "In the Same Place, at the Same Time, and in the Same Way"[2] (all that is reprinted here) began my efforts to state the rules of writing I followed so that others might adapt them for their own use. Were it not for the warm reception accorded this section, which continues to this day, I might not have continued developing this genre.

The eagerness with which these simple prescriptions were greeted led me to understand that basic elements of craftsmanship in social science were not being taught nor observed sufficiently closely to give students (here I indicate not only beginners but middle-aged professors who develop a desire to write) a sufficiently precise idea of how to do their scholarly work. "Rationality in Writing,"[3] by describing how two books were written, was my first effort to elaborate rules for writing, including the rule that there was no right way. That the ways in which a book was written might also have something to do with the content of the book being written, a theme I try to exemplify, brought me closer (though not close enough) to drawing together thought and writing. It was time to try.

During a recent trip to Europe, I visited one of my favorite people, my father-in-law, Edward Cadman. Among other virtues he is a superb craftsman, his hobby (aside from fixing anything) being the repair of ancient clocks. During one of our frequent walks, he inquired about this book, so I described the various chapters. After some thought he came back with, "But they are all about writing; what about reading?" Writing about reading had not occurred to me in quite that way as the subject of an essay. A month later while visiting the Leyden Institute for Law and Public Policy, I wrote "Reading with a Purpose."[9] This volume is dedicated to Edward Cadman because he exemplifies the best in craftsmanship. I am still learning how to work with as much fidelity to my subject matter as he has to his.

The essays in the second section have both common and specific motivations. The motive they share is explicating as carefully and precisely as I can, even at the risk of being overly directive, instructions for essential aspects of the scholar's craft—working with others, using time, and interviewing. Each essay has its own story.

Among the many bits of advice I so freely dispense is making use of time by writing in airplanes and hotel rooms. "The Organization of Time in Scholarly Activities Carried out under U.S. Conditions in Resource-

Rich Research Universities'' was written entirely according to this prescription.[5]

The chapter on interviewing[6] has an instrumental purpose. In contemplating this work, I asked myself what else there was about research and writing I had to contribute. A lifetime of interviewing, reinforced by continuously teaching students, made this subject a natural. But I was not sure whether what I had to teach had not already been taught better by others. Therefore I asked Dean Hammer to work with me by summarizing as a series of prescriptions the prevailing advice in the literature. After several iterations I began qualifying what the experts said and adding my own views. The end result, I hope, is a useful guide to interviewing in short compass. As always it is not just the process itself but the spirit of scholarly enterprise that is meant to animate the interviewing.

''On Collaboration'' describes how I work with other scholars. It seeks to smooth the way for those who would like to try this potentially enriching, but also quite possibly enervating, even destructive, mode of operation.[7]

In the first two sections, I try to transmute the personal into the general. From my own experience, plus my observation of others, I try to generate advice on the craft aspects of scholarship. Their overly prescriptive form is meant to be helpful, if the advice fits. I have often wondered what to do only to discover that advice is either implicit or so general that deducing a course of action is not possible, at least not for me. Hence I have erred on the side of being overly directive. The advice may be inadequate or out of place, but at least the reader knows what it is. One cannot try and fail and learn if one cannot figure out what to try in the first place.

In order to take the curse off of this all too didactic approach, the last section is not partly but wholly personal. No morals are drawn except one, and that is purely personal: When in doubt, do it your own way. What works for others, including me, may not work for you. Craftways have to be your own ways or they will not work for you.

There is more to craftways, in fact, than can be taught or learned directly. Much is a matter of drive or temperament or nuances that may be felt but not necessarily expressed. The injunction to love your work, for instance, sounds more like a command in a totalitarian fantasy than artistic advice; yet it is essential to improving one's craftways. However it comes across better by example, being barely aware that one is being taught.

It is this subliminal lesson that I mean to make emerge from the essays about my family. ''The Richest Boy in Poltava''[8] and ''The Character of Sender Wildavsky and His Family''[9] say something about the milieu from which my work comes. If one looks not at a direct transmission of craft ways—say, a writer in the family—but at subterranean influences—a love of craft—they are there. Thus these pieces are meant to be dialectic, that is, for each to correct the misimpression left by the other. "Things I Never Knew"[10] warns against taking advice that may be good for everyone but you.

Notes

1. (New York: Basic Books, 1971).
2. Ibid., pp. 15–22.
3. *Journal of Public Policy* 1, pt. 1 (February 1981): 125–40.
4. Previously unpublished.
5. Previously unpublished.
6. Previously unpublished.
7. *PS* 19:2 (Spring 1986): 237–48.
8. *Society* 13, no. 1 (November/December 1975).
9. Previously unpublished.
10. *The Revolt against the Masses* (New York: Basic Books, 1971), pp. vii–xi.

Part I
WRITING AND READING

1

In the Same Place, at the Same Time, and in the Same Way

Even if the thought is in you, there is no guarantee it will come out. Between the thought and the deed, there is a vast chasm. That gulf can be bridged only by taking seriously the task of organizing work. In addition to having things to say, the ability to write depends on developing appropriate habits, finding the right kind of place, obtaining useful criticism, learning how to arrange material, working out a suitable physical style, combining teaching and research, overcoming temptations to divert energies, and surmounting the obstacles created by administrative demands.

I cannot overestimate the importance of habit and rhythm: Try to work in the same place, at the same time, and in the same way. Once the rhythm of work begins to take hold, it carries you through fallow periods; it keeps you going through the inevitable descriptive passages that contain nothing new but are essential for the story you are telling or the point you wish to make. Willa Cather's *The Professor's House* contains the best description I know of the impact of a place of residence on a man's work. When the professor moves to another house, he loses his sense of ease and comfort and knowing where he is for the purpose at hand.

There is, I am convinced, no one time of day to write that is good for everyone. I am a morning person myself; if I attempt to write in the evening, it is a sure sign of desperation rather than choice. The important thing is to work at roughly the same time every day so that body and mind expect to be called on and will respond.

I write when I sit and I think when I walk. I like to write for an hour or two and then (hopefully having gotten somewhere) walk and think over the next steps. There is something about releasing the physical energy kept under control while writing that makes it easier to begin again. It is a mistake to push oneself when the flesh is weak and the spirit unwilling.

3

Writing is not only a mental but a physical process in which a sense of touch connects thought with word. In my early college days, I wrote everything out in longhand first and then typed the final draft. Losing the contact of pen on paper, I thought, would stem the flow of ideas. Faced with the necessity of completing four papers in one week, however, I discovered that I could type the initial drafts. Typing saved a lot of time, and there was something about pounding the machine (I have never been able to tolerate electric typewriters because you cannot feel what you are doing) that created the necessary physical contact.

When I became department chairman, I had to change my work method to conform to circumstances in which writing time might be limited to an hour or two a day. There was time to think and read; the difficulty lay in putting together enough consecutive hours to write. If I could knock out a first draft, I would occasionally be able to finish something of essay length. Reluctantly and over some period of time, I gave up my affair with the typewriter and began dictating.

For the contact with the typewriter, I substitute the sensation of sheets of paper appearing whole and clean out of the void. I press heavily with pen in making revisions, so that I feel a little more like a craftsman. After the sheets of paper get so covered with my scribbles that they are virtually illegible except to devoted secretaries, they are retyped and the process of revision continues. New paragraphs are written; old ones are abandoned; whole sections are moved from one place to another; the would-be essay is typed several times more until either I or the subject is exhausted. To compose passages that prove exceedingly recalcitrant, I reestablish contact with the typewriter. The time has come when I can even dictate into a machine and not feel as if I have forever lost touch with real life.

In recent years, freed from the demands of administration, I have returned mostly to writing in longhand. I still like the feel of carving out words on paper, and a weak back makes typing difficult. Now I am about to launch into word processing, where I can use a lap console.

Before studying with Arthur Charles Cole, a historian who lived and breathed research, I did not know how to organize a large piece of work. Notes were stuck in odd places. It was anyone's guess whether they would ever be retrieved. Professor Cole taught me how to work systematically from note cards. These lessons are reviewed in the final chapter.

Writing is a process of self-discovery that sometimes leads you to say more than you knew was in you or carries you far from original intentions. That is why I have learned not to worry about introductions to books or the first few paragraphs of an essay. There is no sense in trying too hard to get them "right," because you do not know what that will be until you finish. The purpose of a beginning is to get you started; when the work is completed, you can go back to the beginning and tell the reader not what you thought you were going to say but what you ended up saying.

Oftentimes you get stuck in the course of writing. You sit at your desk and nothing happens. Sometimes the only thing to do is to leave it alone. But there are other ways. If you are writing a book, some parts always seem easier than others. It helps to gain confidence by turning to something that does write more easily. When one part of a paper seems utterly impossible, others, which had previously appeared just as difficult, seem easier by comparison. Through a process of sequential reduction, you arrive at a point where only a few critical passages remain and there is the incentive of knowing that when these difficulties are overcome the paper will be completed.

I get as much help as I can in improving my work. In Oberlin it was obviously not possible in a four-man department to find people who shared my precise interests. After getting general comments from one or two of my colleagues, I would send preliminary drafts of papers to friends all over the country. At Berkeley I will ordinarily get five or six comments before sending a batch of 20 or 30 to various people who might be interested in the subject and be willing to give me comments. This is a common practice that serves to facilitate communication among scholars. One of the hard things about academic life is that one's friends and colleagues get scattered. Circulating papers not only helps improve the quality but enables me to keep in touch with people I like but rarely get to see.

Writing is a severe discipline. The writer puts himself on the line. His words stand exposed. He is subject to criticism, if not to ridicule. He is alone with himself for long periods when no one is there to provide support. He cannot depend on the surface push of events to carry him along. In his isolation and precariousness, a setback may seem overwhelming. The temptation to withdraw into the self is sometimes irresistible, for it is easy to invent one excuse after another to stop writing. When a scholar has been writing for some time, he is also subject to less obvious temptations to stop writing, less obvious because they flow from previous accomplishments.

The creative years are often spent in obscurity. The scholar, unknown, spends his time working. Then something he writes takes hold. He is called upon to give lectures at distant places. Each trip he takes seems justified at the time by the interest of the locale, the worthiness of the cause, or the attractiveness of the people. The more he talks, however, the less he has to say. He has been using up his intellectual capital, and if he does not watch out his services will become more and more in demand as his thoughts are less and less worth hearing.

My trial came with program budgeting. For a couple of years, it was the rage. Local, state, national, and international bureaucracies had to have it. Being one of the few national critics of program budgeting, I was called upon to go everywhere. No one should believe that I resisted this temptation. For six months I was in full flight. I knew I should stop, but it was hard. Finally I refused outright to discuss program budgeting. The only measure of defense was not to cut down the evil but to eliminate it altogether. The fact that repeated exposure led me to loathe the topic made it a little easier.

There is a Gresham's law—good little projects drive out better big ones—that results from giving in to an insidious form of temptation. There are invitations to contribute articles to symposia, prepare special reports for governmental bodies, and submit papers for publication in leading reviews. The temptation is insidious because there is nothing wrong with the requests. Each proposal is desirable in and of itself; the subject is interesting; the research required is worthwhile; and the scholarly purpose is eminently justifiable. The trouble is that these good little projects represent diversions from the main line of scholarly inquiry. It is so easy to find one's self committed two years in advance to do one little interesting thing after another, so that the whole is, alas, considerably less than the sum of its parts. One defense is simply to say no to everything. A better way, I have found, is to accept only those projects that fit in with longer range scholarly plans. I will take an assignment that promises to teach me something but will reject one that represents a slight variation on what I have done before.

The best way to avoid some kinds of temptations is to give in to others. I seek out projects that have multiple uses. My ideal is to undertake research and writing that will serve as a focus for classroom lectures and seminar discussions. When I am in the first-draft stage, I like to give lectures on the subject of the paper because it helps me think. In effect lectures constitute permission to think in public.

There is a widespread belief that teaching is opposed to research. The more you do of one, supposedly, the less you do of the other. I disagree. Teaching and research belong together. Teaching is more interesting and more valuable when the instructor has done original work and has known the discipline of writing down his thoughts and having them subjected to criticism by his peers. There is no better guarantee of a teacher's interest in his students than that they should be working together on a subject that is of scholarly interest to him. Teaching is an invaluable aid in writing. It helps clarify thoughts and increases fluency. My experience has been that those who take scholarship seriously enough to want to share it with others make the best teachers; writing is, after all, a form of teaching.

Teaching has been an invaluable aid in my research, just as research has enhanced my teaching. One of my books, *Leadership in a Small Town*, was wholly conceived and developed in an undergraduate course. On being told to teach a course on state and local government at Oberlin, I was dismayed because I had scarcely heard of the subject. After reading several texts and various articles in the field, I was appalled. The existing literature was dull and uninformative. It dealt largely with the minutiae of municipal administration and contained numerous cliches like "the superiority of the city manager form of government" without evidence to back them up. I simply could not subject myself and my students to counting manhole covers all semester. In desperation I recalled that two of my friends at Yale, Nelson Polsby and Raymond Wolfinger, were working with Professor Robert Dahl on a community power study of who controlled the decision-making process in New Haven, Connecticut. I sent for their material, read widely in the literature, and decided that students might as well get some contact with the world by finding out how things were done in the town of Oberlin. In the next three years, successive classes in State and Local Government accumulated (and used for its reading lists) numerous papers on how specific decisions were made. We even did a small survey to determine the extent of citizen interest and activity and to compare ordinary citizens with political activists. By that time I found myself involved with the personalities and drama of political events in Oberlin. It was only when preparing for the fourth year of classes that I read through the student material and realized that with another year's work on my part there would be enough to write a book. Working with Alden Small, who had taken the course, taught me a lot I later put to use about working with students on research projects.

If teaching and research may be compatible, there is less reason to be sanguine about the relationship between writing and administration. As chairman of the political science department, with its 50 faculty members, 900 undergraduate majors, 300 graduate students, and 14 secretaries, I soon discovered it was impossible to carry on the intense personal contact required by the job and then leave it for a while in order to read, reflect, or write. The pace of events was too swift. So I tried, with modest success, to set aside mornings for scholarly work. I began early and kept at it until the telephone proved too insistent or my colleagues hunted me out in desperation.

On hectic days it all seemed impossible. Between consulting with my colleagues, coping with a few minor disasters, trying to recruit good people to the faculty, arranging the appropriate coalition for the next department meeting, soothing the outraged and the injured, and trying to invent new educational policies, there was no time for anything else. The worst deprivation however was not the actual time spent on departmental matters, but the diversion of mental energies from scholarly channels. Whereas I used to walk and think about the theoretical problems of my research, I found the latest department crisis preempting my attention.

On better days, with quiet mornings spent reading, writing, or talking to students, I felt that the combination of scholarly thought and administrative action had something to be said for it. The two kinds of activities tire out different parts of the mind and body. You can be exhausted in one and still have energy to carry out the other. They gratify different senses and arouse different anxieties. Harmony among them depends on getting sufficient time to give each its due. They do share one common requisite: unflagging energy. In the end there is the consolation of knowing that the worst that can happen to you as an administrator is to be fired so you will have more time for the main work of your life. And as a postscript, I managed that once as well.

2

Rationality in Writing: Linear and Curvilinear

A long time ago, I received a letter from Rex Stout inviting me to join the Authors' Guild, a letter no doubt sent to all who had books published. I did not join because I did not think of myself as primarily a writer, but as an aspiring scholar who merely set out the results of investigations that, so to speak, wrote themselves. Writing was incidental, not essential. Some years later a similar letter arrived. By then, having spent several hours a day writing most days, I joined. I had become a writer, if not by accomplishment, at least by occupation. Only recently however have I thought of myself as a writer by vocation, as a person who cares about the quality and craft of writing as inseparable from the content of whatever I am trying to communicate. Indeed for me writing has become an integral part of thinking.

I do not know what I think until I have tried to write it. Sometimes the purpose of writing is to discover whether I can express what I think I know; if it cannot be written, it is not right. Other times I write to find out what I know; writing becomes a form of self-discovery. I always hope to learn more than was in me when I started; few feelings compare with the exhilaration of discovering a thought in the writing that was not in the thinking.

Writing should also resonate with its subject matter. Making the form fit the substance, so style reinforces content, is what craftsmanship is about. But the style should also fit the author, for style is a personal signature. In fields where who is writing affects what is written, it should be possible to recognize the author from the style. The danger is that the work might appear idiosyncratic—Smith (or Wildavsky) is at it again—so the subject matter brings little to the finished work. Nothing would be learned except what was in the author; worst of all the author would not have learned anything, and neither would the reader. It is one thing to want to read a piece because of the author and quite another to learn more about the author than the subject.

Books should be crafted. They are in their way like sculptures, hewn, chipped away, shaped from recalcitrant material, imparting a somewhat different cast than was originally intended. Getting more out of yourself than you know, so that the final version reads in part as if it were written by a stranger, reveals writing as a process of discovery.

In another essay (see chapter 5), I have tried my hand at specifying conditions facilitating writing—the importance of habit and habitat (a regular time and place) can hardly be overestimated. Here I would like to venture closer to writing, the mystery that brings form and content together.

Books can be written linearly, straight-on according to plan, with one topic following another in orderly sequence. Books may also be written in curvilinear fashion, much like fitting together the parts of a puzzle except that all the pieces are not available at the beginning but only as one goes along, and the final shape is made up by the pieces instead of being fit into a predetermined form. Immediately I hasten to add that though the process may be curvilinear, the story should be linear, beginning with the statement of a central theme, each chapter related to what went before and what is coming next, the conclusion making it all seem as if it all were planned to fit together from the beginning. Sometimes the book that is published reads the way it was written, but mostly it does not. Its ultimate appearance belies its actual parenthood. In books ontology does not recapitulate phylogeny, rather the reverse, since the full-grown specimen deliberately obfuscates all signs of indiscrete youth. The great bugaboo about books, which I hope to dispel, is that they were always what they became.

I have written both ways—straight on and roundabout—and each has its pleasures and pitfalls. Linear is easier, but it must be done consecutively, the relationship among the parts being retained, so that time is a critical constraint. Curvilinear is more rewarding because of the surprise (astonishment is only a little too strong) at creating something new. Curvilinear is also more correct; it does not confuse the appearance of a scientific article (with its hypotheses, tests, and conclusions all neatly laid out) with the ways in which the mind works or the work was actually carried out. After a brief excursion into linearity, therefore, I will concentrate on curvilinearity.

The Linear Mode

I did not come to England to write *The Private Government of Public Money:*[1] instead I carried with me the note cards that ended up as *Planning and Budgeting in Poor Countries.*[2] While in England I sought to interview a few officials in order to compare British and U.S. budgeting. But they made it so difficult (How could a mere outsider understand their subtle arts?) and they showed so much disdain that I determined to show them. Six months later I had enlisted Hugh Heclo in the cause, had a mountain of interview data, and discovered I had a month left—22 working days—before returning to the United States. We had found out enough for participants to want to tell us more; the question was how to cope with the avalanche of evidence made available toward the end of my stay.

My aim in this book was to use a description of the cut-and-thrust of conflict over expenditures, to illuminate, much as an anthropologist might, the peculiar culture of British central political administration. My fascination with the breed, which motivated the study, would become its central subject. I had also just started a graduate school of public policy and was naturally interested in new institutions for doing and implementing policy analyses. It was easy to develop a straightforward chapter outline beginning with actors in civil service and cabinet society and ending with chapters on new agencies for advancing analyses. By working according to my customary procedures, that is, photocopying all interviews, circling separate thoughts, giving them titles, pasting them on cards, with nine days of effort I was able to arrange four shoe boxes full of what constituted a complete card outline of the first five chapters on tribal relations. The problem was time: Only 13 working days remained. My concern was that the mental interconnections, the nuances, the hard-won empathy necessary to penetrate another culture, to think as they think and to feel as they feel, would be lost if I waited the eight months it would take before I could get back to the subject. Other books were waiting completion in America, books whose coauthors would be available in Berkeley only in the next eight months.[3] How to write what I knew in 13 days?

For reasons not germane to this tale, I was spending three days a week in Oxford and four in London. Therefore I organized a stenographer and a typist plus a dictaphone, both at Nuffield College in Oxford and the Centre of Environmental Studies near Regents Park in London. I worked from 7:00 A.M. to 10:00 P.M. each day (and night). Reading the note cards, I first dictated to the stenographer, then into a tape recorder, after which I took a walk amid the serenity of Regents Park and wrote on park benches in longhand on sheets of yellow foolscap. Then I read a new batch of cards, reordered them, wrote in larger themes, and went at it again.

I needed to write everywhere—on the underground or in line at the post office because there was literally no time to lose. One day the inevitable happened: I left the keys to my London office in Oxford. It was Sunday; the lady who minded the building at Chester Gate would not come for three hours and it was raining. So I sat in the doorway, half in the rain, with smudgy pen and streaky paper, scribbling away.

It was exhausting and it was exhilarating. Sometimes I was so wound up that I walked for an hour-and-a-half down Oxford Street, to Trafalgar Square, to Parliament across the embankment, all the way to my flat at Smith Street off Kings Road in Chelsea.

On the airplane leaving London, with the only copy in my hands, I barely corrected it and then renumbered some 240 pages. It was all a blur, but by the time I landed in San Francisco, I knew that the telltale signs of working from within a culture had been preserved.

The manuscript was copied and sent to Hugh Heclo, who probably spent more time rewriting and reinterviewing than if he would have had to start from scratch. It took him, magically, eight months. By then I returned, worked with my collaborator, and the book was completed in the normal way.

Even now I worry about misleading readers into thinking the extraordinary is ordinary, that I write on the run. Not so! Whatever I have done has been the product of steady effort, something each day rather than everything in a few days. Correction moreover is the norm, not the exception. Rewriting is as (or more) important than writing. Once a draft is done, its creation is the occasion for destruction and eventual (five to eight drafts are usual) reconstruction.

Never before or since have I written so much so rapidly in so short a time. It is not a method I would recommend. Usually I write 2 to 6 pages, not 15 to 30, a day, and I have never wanted to repeat the experiment. But in its time, it was right for me to write as if there were no tomorrow, because there was not.

The Curvilinear Mode

If I wrote about British political administration to set out what I thought I knew, I wrote about policy analysis in order to discover what I thought. *Speaking Truth to Power* is pure rationalization: I took what I had done in separate essays, studied them, and tried to invent general concepts under which they would comfortably fit. A somewhat less blatant way of saying the same thing is that I sought to bring out explicitly ideas common to various studies that were, presumably, implicit in them.

In this special sense, all books are rationalizations designed to present work the way it ought to look, not the way it looked at the time. In publishing a piece, one would not normally present the prose historically, following the work as it was done, leading the reader down false paths and blind alleys, giving equal space to hypotheses rejected and accepted, thereby exhausting the reader long before the subject. Though a book may look the same whether it were written from the top down, as if I knew what it would be about from the start, or from the bottom up, learning what it was about as I went along, the movement of the mind, so to speak, is markedly different.

I was often put off by philosophy of science because it seemed so remote from anything I might imagine anyone like myself doing. (My rule was simplicity itself; at the first mention of Ohm's law, close the book.) But now that exposition of rules for codifying conclusions has been replaced by descriptions of how work is done, as historians replace logicians, scientists emerge suspiciously like the rest of us. A convenient mode of presenting research results in journals, which is what we say of our work when it is dead and done, should not be confounded with the confused concatenations of its creation. The imposition of order on recalcitrant material, which we optimistically call knowledge, is a sometimes thing, hard won, temporary, and artificial, like the rest of civilization.

It all started when I was asked to consider becoming dean of a new school of public affairs, a school whose character was not determined nor its procedures weighted down with the accumulation of past practices. Fortunately Basic Books had asked me to collect my essays, which on rereading I discovered to be largely concerned with public policy. That literally is how I found out what my main interest was. But by public policy, I mostly meant studies of how governmental policies were made, not, except for the structure of political institutions, what they ought to be. Perforce the usual faculty meetings and curriculum committees were explorations in what policy analysis might become, not what I thought I knew it already was.

After the first two years, when it appeared that the Graduate School of Public Policy was likely to remain a viable institution, I gradually grew aware of a certain anomaly in my relationship to this enterprise—I had never actually done a policy analysis. Suppose some students asked me, if I presumed to be so bold as to participate in imposing a curriculum on them, whether I had ever analyzed a public policy? Suppose I asked myself whether I might not be a better teacher or administrator if I had firsthand experience as a policy analyst. The answer was as embarrassing as it was self-evident, so I set out to remedy these deficiencies through self-education.

Three years later by accepting every chance that came my way, I could be said, by some stretch of the imagination, to have done something like policy analyses in a number of different areas—libraries, health, recreation, and education. When an opportunity presented itself to develop an alternative to the income tax deduction as a method of support for charity,

I seized on it by working with a student, not only to give the client what he asked, but to do so by the book in the manner prescribed by the school.[4] Nonetheless a number of disparate analyses do not a book make.

Along the way I had continued an earlier interest in organizational change, focusing this time on difficulties in evaluating public policies and acting on these studies. Error correction was not easy. While involved in an action-research project in the city of Oakland, I had become aware of the great gap between policy ideas and program implementation. Thus the thought took root that since an organization was a creator and tester of policy hypotheses (if this were done, that would follow), its normative character should be conceived as the detection and correction of error. A concern with error, however, is not the same as a conceptual framework for placing policy analysis within the context of organizational life.

A still earlier interest in budgetary processes had led to consideration of collective calculations (How might congeries of complex choices be made?) and from there ineluctably to national planning (Is it desirable to make comprehensive calculations of proposed policies for years ahead?). But the debates over planning always appeared intertwined with capitalism versus socialism or faith versus reason or anything and everything except what made sense as policy analysis. Could I make these shopworn statements speak to issues of public policy?

At this point in order to follow the implications of these findings, I accepted an invitation to lecture in Sweden and Norway. Gradually extending the range of comparisons among policies and called on to be more explicit to foreign audiences, I realized that there was a pattern to be perceived: When change was inside people, like improving cognition or following healthier habits, public policies often failed, but when change was in the government, like equalizing expenditures per pupil or spending more proportionately on welfare and less on "warfare," government often succeeded. Were this so, were there congenital defects in government as well as market failures in the economy, retreating from unsupportable objectives was both desirable and inevitable. It was desirable because promise and performance had to be connected, and it was inevitable because no one wants to be branded as a failure in public. Indeed one thing did lead to another; forms of escape from failure helped explain the pattern in which new clients who could achieve objectives replaced old ones who could not (namely, deinstitutionalization of the mentally ill and decriminalization of marijuana), and change for its own sake increased as decisionmakers sought to manipulate the one resource over which they had the most control, their own organizations.

But, why, since knowledge grew and people were better educated, was collective failure increasing along with individual competence? The pessimism about public policy cried out for explanation and if possible for counteraction, lest democracy go down with it. Suddenly in the midst of answering questions about how policies in one sector impinged on those in another, it all became clear: Policies were becoming their own causes. As government grew, large problems suggested larger solutions that bulked so large in their sectors that they became the major source of future problems. As policies proliferated they began bumping into each other in unexpected ways, increasing the number, variety, and range of consequences. Professionals knew more, but the gap between that and what they needed to know grew even larger. Whereas knowledge increased arithmetically, consequences of policies colliding increased geometrically. We did know more, but our knowledge had not expanded so much as big government.

Enough. It is not my intention to rewrite this book but only to explain where I was when I started, that is, thinking the book was over when it had hardly begun.

Easy, is it not? All I had to do was put together (I do not say write because my first thought was one of assembling the existing pieces) a book. It would begin with articles I had done on policies—health, education, charity, the environment, and the rest—followed by drawing inferences about the retreat from objectives and policy as its own cause. Q.E.D. or at least finis.

The only thing wrong was that it would not write, and I did not like it because it was dull and it was forced. The dullness came from having to read so much detail without being told what it was all about until the stories were over. Moreover I found myself forcing the material to tell all about policy analysis when it wanted to tell only part of the story.

What to do? When in doubt, go with what you have. Spreading out in front of me the papers dealing directly with the causes and consequences of policy making, it became apparent that there were substantial gaps. For one thing most social welfare policies were missing. There was no discussion of food stamps or social security nor mention of the move from categorical to cash grants, indexing against inflation, "grandfathering" old clients into new programs, or "upgrading" so everyone received higher benefits. At the same time, the tone in speaking about each program was more pessimistic than I felt was deserved by the effort as a whole. The sixties were not, in my opinion, a disastrous decade, yet there was no denying the failure of most programs to achieve objectives set for them.

Leaving the reconciliation of this apparent contradiction for another time, I sought to leaven the cake of discontent (it looks sweet from the outside but tastes sour on the inside) by including discussion of programs that worked. Students at the Graduate School of Public Policy in Berkeley were offered imaginary prizes for what it turned out were nonexistent policies. Those I thought of were either too old, like adult education, or too different, like civil rights and voting laws, or too suspect, like everything else. Believe me, I tried. Then as so often happened before, reading budgetary literature, more out of ancient habit than current interest, reminded me of something so obvious it had not come to mind: In the early 1960s, expenditures on welfare had been about 20 percent of the federal budget with defense around 45 percent, but by the mid-1970s, the relationship in real terms had been reversed. Here was an opportunity to show success and increase coverage, all within a single chapter. The success would be reversing the financial effort between welfare and defense, and the coverage would include the major programs responsible for the increase in expenditures on social welfare. Easier said than done. It took a year for four research assistants to compile capsule histories of some two dozen programs. Up till the end, we held our breaths to discover whether we could create common patterns accounting for this radical restructuring of national priorities. Looking for more complex considerations, it took a while to realize that simple but strongly held beliefs—it is better to include the deserving than exclude the undeserving; benefits may be raised but not lowered—go a long way when widely held and consistently applied to explaining the vast increase in expenditure.

So what? So the whole thing still did not fit together. If it were to be an analytic history of current U.S. public policy, it still was not nearly inclusive or detailed enough. If it were to say what policy analysis was about, it had to be organized by categories appropriate to its subject. Yet for years I had resisted direct discussion of the thing-in-itself both because discussion had seemed fruitless and because the doing seemed so much more substantial than the explaining. It was time to choose.

Whenever my colleagues and I began our courses by asking, "What is policy analysis?" or what proved to be worse, "what is a problem?" student anxiety rose alarmingly. The classroom crackled with tension. It was as if students felt that the faculty were withholding something vital— the strange and simple secret of analysis—which we must have known (because students could not learn it). Yet our promise of better things to come, though designed of course to soothe the raging beast, was borne out by experience. Students did learn to do analysis; and if our observation and their job experience were any guide, students not only *felt* but *were* more competent. What was it then that could be learned but not explained, that all of us could sometimes do but none of us could ever define (at least to anybody else's satisfaction)?

A first clue came from an unusual aspect of our teaching experience: Policy analysis was better taught backward. Instead of beginning with formulation of a problem, consideration of alternative solutions, development of criteria, application of criteria to data, and so on, student work improved when exercises went the other way. The best way to begin learning was to apply clear criteria to perfect data for choosing among existing alternative programs, go on to create criteria and discover data, make up alternatives, and after numerous trials, formulate a problem that could be solved at the very end. Why did anxiety decline and confidence rise when entering through the back door? Possibly formulating the problem was more like the end than the beginning of analysis.

Problem finding is analogous to inventing or theorizing. In invention the task is not to compile a list of all unfulfilled human needs (or the shorter list of those that deserve fulfillment), but to connect what might be wanted with what can be provided. The prizes in science go to those who choose what turn out to be interesting and solvable problems. So, too, in policy analysis, the most creative calculations concern finding problems for which solutions might be attempted. No wonder then that students go into shock the first week if they are (in effect) asked to create original social inventions. Their teachers cannot do that either. Since policy analysis presumes creativity (the injunction to be creative is notoriously unhelpful), a subject about which almost nothing is known, our inability to teach analysis directly is easy to understand. It is also difficult to remedy, for if policies are increasingly their own causes, problem solving may be a less accurate observation than problem succession. And if problems are less likely to be solved than superseded, perhaps they might be thought of as perennial.

The last three paragraphs are taken from the introduction to *Speaking Truth to Power*, which is appropriate because I was writing that to explain to myself what policy analysis was about. Usually I write the first part last in order to introduce the book I actually wrote instead of the numerous potential others that might have been written but were not. Here however I wanted to see what kind of book to write, so my capacity to make the contents cohere would test the concept. Clearly compared to the earlier confusion, the book was to be about policy analysis: But what was policy analysis?

The Introduction still sounds like what it started to be, a long shaggy-dog story, always about to tell the reader exactly what analysis is, leading imperceptibly away from a denotative definition—it is this or that and nothing else—to an understanding that an applied subfield, which must draw on whatever is appropriate in the circumstances, cannot be so circumscribed. But if that detour led out of a blind alley, to what did it lead?

Groping, groping. Just now the thought crossed my mind that the book must always have been about objectives. But this is my current explanation, not a historical description. The ideas came from the activity of asking the same question as everyone else: Why is there so much failure to achieve objectives in public policies? If objectives of public policy were immutable, how was learning possible? If all that was done was to find more efficacious means to fixed ends, failure would always be in how things were done, never in what we were trying to do. If mistakes were inevitable, even desirable to speed learning, as all my experience cried out, why should objectives be inviolable? It took time to understand that under some circumstances retreat was right. After all, changing what we ought to want, educating our preferences, so to speak, is a moral enterprise.

Most discussions of public policy are organized around the clash between markets and politics. The great issues are supposed to be whether government itself should do things directly or whether society should rely on spontaneous interaction in economic markets. For a long time discussions of laissez-faire versus central bureaucratic command left me cold. These classic descriptions did not resonate with what I knew about public policy. Even when government controlled an activity, it had to decide whether to lay down general rules within which the people involved would pursue their own interests or to specify step-by-step the proper procedure, monitoring each and every transaction. This very issue for example comes up when the federal government chooses between monitoring millions of hospital charges or establishing a cost constraint within which hospitals must operate. Even socialist societies must choose between general rules and detailed regulations.

If we think of planning as an intellectual or cognitive activity—figuring out the right thing to do as if society had a single mind—it is apparent that analysis partakes of planning. If we think of democratic policies as repeated give and take between independent interests, then markets and politics, bidding and bargaining, have more in common than is commonly supposed. The criterion of choice in politics and markets is not being right or correct, as in solving a puzzle, but agreement based on interaction among partially opposed interests. Rather than use terms like planning versus markets, which might encourage stereotypes, I deliberately chose more abstract terms—social interaction—people mixing it up (as in politics and economics) versus intellectual cogitation (putting people through paces worked out in advance by a great mind). Naturally neither acting without thinking of the collective consequences, as in social interaction, or thinking of what is good for everyone without asking anyone (as in intellectual cogitation) is desirable. My preference is for cogitation (that is, policy analysis) not to replace but to restrain interaction.

It was this distinction between cogitation and interaction (see Table 2.1)

TABLE 2.1.
Alternative Styles of Policy Analysis

	Social Interaction	Intellectual Cogitation
Institutions	Markets and politics	Planning
Calculations	Parital	Comprehensive
Calculators	Many minds interacting	Single-minded deciding
Decision making	Exchange and bargaining	Comprehending and deciding
Error	Correction	Avoidance
Criteria	Agreement	Right
Administration	Reactions	Orders

that set up the second set of tensions around which the book was organized. Though I soon discovered that distinction had recently been made by Charles E. Lindblom in his seminal study on *Politics and Markets* (Basic Books, 1978), I was more relieved to find a meeting of the minds than worried about being anticipated. Now I knew I had a book.

Once I had clarified my understanding of objectives and resources, the first section of the book fell into place. It would begin by setting this relationship straight and go on to show how failure to do so was responsible for the faults of the public policies under consideration. If it were wrong to do things just because one could, it was also wrong to promise without hope of performance. And if treating this type of tension were useful, I reasoned, there might be others around which to organize the rest of the book.

I did not want to write a how-to-do-it book, which could never go into sufficient detail, but a how-to-understand-it book, which would welcome people into the field without specialized preparation.

Earlier on I had recognized the need to say something about the place of economic theory in policy analysis. I also wanted the book to have a general readership. The first mention of cost curves or use of geometry, let alone regressions, would be the end of that hope. My pedagogical purpose was to imbed the economic theory in an argument of some sort about public policy so the reader would pick up what was necessary almost in passing, hopefully without realizing he was being taught. Two subjects were prime candidates—cost-benefit analysis and opportunity costs—the one applying economic criteria to public programs, the other containing the key assumptions in economy theory. I considered the idea that cost and worth were measured by alternatives forgone as central to economic thought. Since I also wanted to stress citizenship, it was important to have a concept applicable to deciding what one gives up for what one gets. Therefore I asked an economically sophisticated graduate student; Bruce Wallin, to prepare preliminary papers on both subjects.

Cost-benefit did not pan out because I did not understand it well enough to go beyond what I had written a decade before, but opportunity costs did. When we decided to contrast opportunity costs with the competing concept of merit wants, which asserts that some needs are so superior they should be subsidized, basic differences in doctrine shot out in bold relief. Lo and behold as the argument unfolded, the interactive assumptions of opportunity costs, which approach objectivity by bidding and bargaining, contrasted well with planning by cogitation to figure out and enforce ideas of the meritorious. By then I was able to understand that cogitation versus interaction was also the main theme of my earlier work on federalism (a single unit cogitating versus many interacting) and on environmental policy, where conflict involved a rejection of the belief that markets fairly measured values. The second section had taken shape.

How much cogitation and how much interaction? That depends. Those who enjoy the outcomes of interactive processes, well positioned with votes in political arenas or dollars in economic markets, are likely to want more of the same, and those who do badly are more inclined to restructure these relationships. What is to be held inviolate and what is subject to change is of the utmost importance in an endeavor where ability to define the problem takes one a long way toward a solution. Since resources, including time, attention, and knowledge are limited, choices about change have to be made.

Policy analysis is based on skepticism, but since not everything can be comprehended or altered at once, it depends on a substratum of dogma. Though it is easy to delude oneself into believing that a self-critical activity like policy analysis questions everything, experience shows that most things have to be taken for granted most of the time.

How was the tension between dogma and skepticism conceived? It was in the air, all right, but it was not yet in my mind as an essential element of policy analysis. My choices began with elimination and ended with accretion. As usual I tried my substantive policy papers and decided that they all fit so well with the strain between skepticism and dogma there was no way to choose among them. They were right in general but wrong in particular because they did not advance the argument about analysis depending on the ability to focus on a few key variables, which meant that most had to be ignored. If everything were up for grabs all the time, neither citizen nor analyst would be able to function in a recognizable universe. Accretion began with "The Self-Evaluating Organization," where I first understood that the requirements of organizational maintenance, without which it could do neither good nor evil, were at odds with the analytic imperative to evaluate and change. Trying out a model of the organization wholly devoted to altering its policies by monitoring its own activities, I concluded that there were strong tendencies pushing it to end up much like the error-suppressing agencies it was designed to supplant. If the ideal organization were recognizing and correcting errors, drawing the line between internal maintenance and external adaptation was crucial. Thus the section on dogma versus skepticism would begin with the dilemma of self-evaluation.

While I was considering these ideas, the 1976 presidential elections, with all the questions about Jimmy Carter, came along. Looking into the matter with Jack Knott, I discovered that Carter's distinctive characteristic was not his policy preferences but his views on proper procedures for policy making. He believed that policies ought to be simple, predictable, and uniform more than he believed in their content. In a word he was all skepticism and no dogma. Willing to take little for granted, he favored comprehensive solutions, from ground zero, in order to leave nothing out. I argued that he drew the line so severely as to be unworkable. But whether the president were wrong or not, the article was right for showing that the dividing line between dogma and skepticism was as current as the day's newspapers.

An earlier debate on who rules in U.S. communities, in which I had participated,[5] was also about the ability of citizens to influence their government. The pluralist side maintained there was considerable ability because citizens were able to modify marginally the way things were; the elitist side said citizens lacked influence because they could not change the life chances of people. There is a world of difference between a current cross-sectional view that accepts the past and asks how it might be modified by the next move and a historical view that asks why some people are better off than others in total resources. Similarly I saw that the perennial fact-value controversy was about the extent of change: Those groups least satisfied with the status quo insisted that more values be altered in their favor before they would be willing to certify certain facts. All these controversies, it became apparent, were about how much to accept as given versus how much to change in public policy.

In a democracy there is not much point in identifying change unless citizens are able to play a part in it. All along my interest in analysis has been subsidiary to a concern with the success of democratic institutions. Unless citizens become analysts, able to make intelligent choices by relating their resources to their objectives as patrons of the post office or users of medical services, they will not be able to make sense out of their public lives. I was interested in how citizens might participate continuously as part of public policy rather than merely in the initiation stages. Thus after many tries, I wrote a chapter on "Citizens as Analysts," thereby completing the section on dogma versus skepticism.

However convoluted the construction of this section may appear, it does not quite compare with what happened. In the beginning, you see, I thought the section was going to be about error detection and correction. Unfortunately this theme was in everything I wrote so that any section to illustrate it, beyond "The Self-Evaluating Organization," in which it was featured, proved to be arbitrary. Nevertheless I tried many combinations before allowing "error" to permeate the book as a whole.

I was still left with those pesky papers actually pretending to provide the policy analysis the book was ostensibly about. This was to be a book about policy analysis through analysis, which, without examples of analysis, might be too much like Hamlet without the prince. Parceled out among the three sections every which way, I tried virtually all combinations; they were not badly out of place but they did not quite fit. From time to time, the fleeting thought that they might go together passed my mind only to pass out again for lack of a way of connecting them.

Nothing to do then but to take the hard-won three sections—resources versus objectives, social interaction versus intellectual cogitation, and dogma versus skepticism—and rewrite the Introduction to see what I had. It worked. Moreover it turned out that in dealing with difficulties about which something ought and could be done, which we call policy analysis, solutions had to be proposed before one could understand whether there were problems.

Problems are not so much found as created. Since there are no rules for creativity, policy analysis had to be an art form. Seeking symmetry I immediately became aware that a major aspect of policy analysis, discussed endlessly with our students, namely, the aspects of craftsmanship that made it persuasive to others, had been omitted.

The easy way out was to write a conclusion called "Analysis as Craft" paralleling the Introduction by then named "Analysis as Art," which would highlight the craft aspects that had heretofore been overlooked. Without the chapters covering analysis, however, there was not much to say about craft. So then I knew that the fourth section had to include policy analyses, with emphasis on how these were crafted.

The vision of a book was there; the contents were in place; only the Aristotelian virtues were missing—unity, harmony, and symmetry. Three times I went through the manuscript word for word, trying to make its concepts leap out from the page connecting the thoughts and the sections, polishing, pruning, rearranging.

The time had come to circulate copies to colleagues, encouraging criticism, seeking advice. Helpful comments were received and changes made. Still it did not hang together as it should. Conversation with Robert Merton, whose detailed critique was invaluable, convinced me that more connectives were required. It was asking too much of the Introduction to hold the whole thing together. With more than a little misgiving in view of the work involved, I decided there was nothing to do but write substantial introductions to each of the four sections. To the classic but still compelling advice—"tell 'em what you're going to tell 'em, tell 'em what you told 'em"—I had added "tell 'em again as you go along."

With heavy heart I had to consider how to write introductions to the four sections in words I had not used before. The process was painful. On craftsmanship in analysis and on dogma versus skepticism, I had written so little that new essays were required, teasing out explicitly what was implicit. Resources versus objectives was easier because there were always more examples of misaligning ends and means. But I had said so much about cogitation and interaction that I was stymied. My prose sounded like what I said before except that every other sentence was written backward. That would not do. If an idea resonates with the world, I believe evidence of it should appear in daily life. Sure enough, on a trip to the West, held over in Denver, I picked up a discarded copy of the *Rocky Mountain News* and found a plethora of policies in which interactive versus cognitive modes were competing.

Inevitably further rearrangement was required. Every book is finally finished ten times, and this was no exception. Whatever I say now will still fail to do justice to the dead ends and detours, the endless circling back, abandonment and reconsideration that, without being quite it, became the thing that was done.

Actually the fate of this book and this essay about it may be intertwined in more ways than one: The book attacks the prevailing paradigm of rationality. The obsession with objectives is only part of the many pitfalls of the paradigm of rationality. Have objectives; rank them; choose the highest ranking. What is wrong with it? Everything. The paradigm suggests that objectives matter apart from resources, whereas policy analysis must make them inseparable. Its image of a hierarchy of objectives suggests they all fit together like Chinese boxes, whereas the order and extent of implementation affect everything that happens afterward. Early choices preempt later ones. The interconnection of super-and-subordinate objectives, moreover, makes error detection difficult—How can one separate effects from a seamless web of causality?—and error correction virtually impossible—Who would want to change anything if everything has to be changed? Comprehensive cogitation by a single mind at a single point in time not only places impossible burdens on knowledge, it also does not make use of evolutionary understanding by many minds interacting. Retrospection (as retrospective rationalization is called in the book) retrofits the past, so to speak, in order to accommodate the future that one is learning to prefer. If there is a rationality in writing, it is not only of the linear sort but also of the curvilinear kind in which the author fails the sobriety test more than once before putting together the pieces so they look like they always were arranged in a straight line.

Notes

1. *The Private Government of Public Money: Community and Policy inside British Political Administration,* with Hugh Heclo (London: Macmillan; Berkeley and Los Angeles: University of California Press, 1973).
2. *Planning and Budgeting in Poor Countries,* with Naomi Caiden (New York: Wiley, 1974). Each book has a different significance. This one led to other things: The necessity of comparing budgetary processes in rich and poor countries gave me hope of doing the same around the world. (See *Budgeting: A Comparative Theory of Budgetary Processes* [Boston: Little, Brown and Co., 1974]) and deepened my interest in national economic planning, which helped generate the *Speaking Truth to Power: The Art and Craft of Policy Analysis* (Boston: Little, Brown and Co., 1979).
3. *Implementation: How Great Expectations in Washington Are Dashed in Oakland; or Why It's Amazing That Federal Programs Work at All,* with Jeffrey L. Pressman; (Berkeley: University of California Press, 1973) and *The Budgeting and Evaluation of Federal Recreation Programs or Money Doesn't Grow on Trees,* with Jeanne Nienaber (New York: Basic Books, 1973).
4. David Good and Aaron Wildavsky, "A Tax by Any Other Name: The Donor-Directed Automatic Percentage Contribution Bonus, a Budget Alternative for Financing Government Support of Charity," *Policy Sciences* 7 (1976): 251–59.
5. Aaron Wildavsky, *Leadership in a Small Town* (Totowa, N.J.: Bedminster Press, 1964).

3

Reading with a Purpose

Recent literature on reading is overwhelmingly devoted to increasing speed—faster and faster—while hopefully maintaining comprehension. As the publication of books and articles, even good ones, proceeds apace, thought is devoted to the task, no doubt forlorn, of helping the perennially overwhelmed reader to keep up. Speed reading (referring to such presumed exemplars as former President John F. Kennedy) enjoys a continuing vogue. Personally I have nothing against such endeavors; by all means let those who can do so try to increase the number of pages they read, keeping comprehension constant, in a given time.

Nevertheless I believe the emphasis on speed is fundamentally misplaced, not because it is wrong to read more rapidly but because prior (and far more important) considerations—*what* to read and *how* to read it for *which* purpose—are thereby neglected. Reading the wrong things quickly is a much greater waste than reading the right ones slowly.

To the contrary our aim should be to *read the right material ever more slowly*. Selection, not speed, is crucial. By isolating the small amount of material that is crucial to our purpose, we increase creativity efficiently, for we are then better able to make much out of little. In other words this is called theorizing or making an argument or thinking through a subject, that is, playing with and securing a more coherent and powerful arrangement among a small body of concepts.

When one abandons the assumption of having already selected the right type and amount of material to read, a whole new range of subjects comes into view. Scanning, winnowing, focusing, in short, selection, become crucial. Selection, it immediately becomes apparent, depends on purpose; purpose in turn should have some influence on how the material is read.

Countering Selection Bias

All perception is selective. Selecting some items means excluding other items. Reading with a particular purpose in mind means that other purposes cannot be served. Before proceeding to consider how to be more selective, therefore, it is worthwhile considering how to protect oneself against the worst effects of tunnel vision.

No rule for selection is likely to be perfect. Nor should it be, for the price of perfection is likely to involve such fussing with the effort to formulate a precise cutting rule that, as the idiom goes, the game is not worth the candle. Nor can it be. For one thing, as Allan Newell has demonstrated in a seminal essay, generality (covering a wide range of instances) and power (discriminating one instance from another) are at odds.[1] One cannot (and therefore should not try to) square the circle. Similarly Ron Heiner has demonstrated that regularity, like predictability, originates in the pervasive uncertainty of life.[2] Rather than seek an unobtainable precision in coping with an incredibly uncertain environment, with a high probability of being wrong, people seek general rules that work well enough in most cases but not necessarily too well in any single one. Thus things one ought to read are bound to be omitted by whatever general rule is invoked. What to do?

Put yourself in the way of random choice. Read a good selection of book reviews such as the *Times Literary Supplement*—my choice especially because it is done in another country and is therefore likely to counter national biases (were I in England, I would choose a U.S. or continental review). The same principle applies to journals that give broad coverage to reviews, such as the *American Political Science Review* or the *Journal of Economic Literature*. Subscribe to or get on the mailing list of institutions of quality that publish paragraph summaries or short essays summarizing arguments in the book. The Brookings Institution, Resources for the Future, National Bureau of Economic Research, and the American Enterprise Institute put out readable summaries of work in public policy and politics. I like to be on the mailing lists of faraway places because they give access to the odd piece one would otherwise never have seen. Periodic visits to journal rooms of libraries enable one to rummage through journals in many fields to catch a title (help others by putting key words into your titles!) or better still, an abstract that may have something of interest. Try book stacks in libraries, dipping in here and there to catch sight of what one may have missed.

Reviewing articles for journals (volunteer if necessary) not only reveals trends in new work but also provides reading (and footnotes) that one might otherwise have overlooked. Reading manuscripts for other people, besides sharpening critical skills and making one aware of common errors, brings across one's desk a wider variety of research. Sending one's manuscripts to others in the spirit of reciprocity will yield suggestions for further reading.

Such relationships do not arise automatically; they must be cultivated. Some people do not like to read for others, or they take so long, the need has passed. Creating a network is full of errors and trials. But trying and persisting, absent ability to predict who will be both forthcoming and effective, is the only way. The ability to suffer and overcome disappointment is essential for those who wish to broaden their horizons. No doubt putting himself ''in harm's way'' explains why Don Quixote encountered so many adventures at the cost of so often being embarrassed.

Being a reader, that is, a person who loves to read, helps to randomize reading. One is more likely to pick up almost anything almost anywhere, and it is precisely in these unexpected places that the valuable example or reference is likely to appear.

Reading at random can, however, resemble being at sixes and sevens, that is, discombobulated, so it must also be limited, especially by those devoted to reading almost anything irrespective of subject matter. I cannot say how much time should be spent countering the effects of purposeful reading (see my essay on the uses of time for some suggestions). One way to do this is by feel, reading at random so long as one is making progress reading with a purpose. This is my way. Another way might be to set aside 10 percent or so of one's reading-for-research time. My sense is that while it is desirable to think about and act on the uses of time for scholarly endeavor, it is undesirable to do this by rote, thereby making research more mechanical than a creative process should be.

There are two contrary conditions under which randomized reading is especially important—when one's main project is going well and when it is not. When one cannot figure out what to do, when the creative juices appear to congeal, solidifying instead of flowing, random reading may get things going again. Since one does not know what one needs, one may as well put out random probes. When things go well, when in hot pursuit as if one will never stop or could never be wrong, random reading is a good corrective. There is more out there of importance than one knows, some of which might give one pause.

Going against the flow makes sense, however, only if there is a flow. To depart from routine, there needs to be a routine. Countering bias makes sense only against a background of selection.

In Search of Theory

Thinking back to graduate school days, I read incessantly from morning until night. But what was the meaning of it all? The lines swam before my eyes, a sea of run-on sentences, seemingly without end. All those words, words, words everywhere but, or so it then appeared, not a phrase of comprehension. Drowning in words seemed a possible fate.

Incessantly the key to it all was dangled before us. From all sides the word came from on high. The secret had apparently been revealed to a favored or gifted few (I could not tell which). Honored these scholars certainly were, deserving they might well be, but accessible to us they were not. Oh we could on occasion speak with them. At such times however when the dreaded subject came up, they who were otherwise so verbose became strangely reticent. They could barely bring themselves to utter its name, as if modesty forbade their association with so holy a subject. This combination of communication with reluctance, of course, only increased our (mis)apprehension. Were we able to grasp this Holy Grail, all honors would be ours. Yet we graduate students faced what appeared to us as an insuperable double barrier: Even if we were somehow able to pull out this social science Excalibur, this sword of scholarship that would cut a swath through all the mysteries that lay before us, how would we ever know that we had indubitably, in fact, in real life, done so?

In political science was the word, and the word was theory, pronounced reverently, growing larger with the telling—theory, THEORY—only to recede wistfully into the distance as soon as it came into focus. Always alluring, forever, except for the favored few, unreachable. Gradually it dawned on us that if having knowledge of theory were akin to predestination—either you had it or you did not—there was no point in worrying about it or studying for it. Sensing that theory explained whatever was worth explaining but unable to figure out what form it took (a common put-down at the time was to say that some work lacked theory or that someone would not know a theory if he ran into one), we retreated to something admittedly less satisfactory but eminently more practical, namely, who said what. If we could neither recognize nor create theory, we could pass our doctoral exams by telling our professors what the greats and near-greats whose books had been assigned to us had said.

I have deliberately darkened these observations in order to highlight the difficulties of reading when one does not know what to look for. To be sure we were told about and encouraged to read about theories and theorizing. There were to be axioms, definitions, and propositions. We were indeed to test our and others' hypotheses against facts. A theory was a tautology, true only by definition unless it could be refuted. Much was made of operationalizing variables so they could be related to observable phenomena. The normative and empirical realms were distinguished, not well but not too badly. All to the good. If one poked beneath the surface, it was even possible to extract emerging doctrines from Quine and Popper that all facts were theory laden, that observations took their meaning from the theories in which they were embedded. This understanding made one more sophisticated without enabling the beginner to locate the specks of golden theory amid the effluvia in what he was reading.

Certain observations were left out. Much social science is descriptive, an effort to establish rather than to explain social facts. This does not render it useless but makes a search for theory hopeless. Much social science is defective, with large holes in logic, a product of poor craftsmanship. Much social science is discursive, containing scattered insights, which one might think of as partial, possible relationships divorced from anything like a full context. Other works are more but not completely systematic; thus they depend for understanding on a tradition of assumptions and definitions that are neither fully shared—there are rival traditions—nor wholly explicated.

Now I hope the difficulties facing the would-be intelligent reader are more apparent: The reader cannot take existing theory for granted. Rather his task is to make theory out of disparate and disconnected material. This is a formidable task, which is one reason there is so little readily available for the taking. Theory cannot just be picked up; it has to be searched for, chiseled, shaped, pounded, reorganized, and reoriented. Creating coherence out of existing bits of theory is like getting an inside straight in poker.

Theorizing is a creative act. Whether one is asserting that a theory of a kind exists (how remarkable!) or inventing one that claims to be new (thus running afoul of the encapsulated wisdom of the ages—if new, not true; if true, not new), one gets into trouble whichever way one goes.

Exhortations to theorize raise anxiety without providing guidance. It might help if attaining some sense of theory were considered the end, not the beginning, of study. In this context going to the safe cognitive anchorage of simple "author says" has its point. Beginners pay their dues by learning what their predecessors have said. The sense of awe is diminished with familiarity.

There is more that can be done, just not enough. The apprentice reader-cum-theorizer can try to develop the spirit of active reading. How does what this author says compare with what others say? Why do they choose somewhat different objects for explanation? Why do they employ different explanatory (independent) variables or give similar ones different emphases? Challenging the text is worthwhile but like most of this advice, a lot easier to say than for the beginner to do.

There is a way of coming to grips with, and comparing authors on, related subjects that can be learned by practice. I call it writing as a form of reading.

Writing as an Aid to Reading

Writing is an essential aid to reading. Only by writing down what one thinks one knows can one figure out (1) whether one knows it and (2) what one does not yet know. An awful lot of time is spent reading repetitious material because one has not learned by writing that one already knows it. Contrariwise it is easy to pass by new material that one thinks one knows or is not worth knowing because without writing, writing short enough to reread, one does not perceive its connection to one's existing corpus of knowledge.

As Herbert Simon demonstrated in his by-now classic of the watchmakers parable[3] and as Charles Lindblom and David Braybrook argued so persuasively in their *A Strategy for Decision*[4], starting from the beginning every time, as if all decisions had to be made over again, is exhausting and ineffective. Far better to begin with a base, add segments, and then modify at the margin. Converted into instructions for reading, the incremental approach suggests getting a quick fix—finding a textbook or two and perhaps a few review articles, if they exist, writing out and reorganizing their basic propositions, reading, modifying, and repeating the sequence.

In general we read too much and write too little. Writing while reading, writing to improve reading, is far more efficacious than racing through a body of literature in an undisciplined manner.

Substituting for something students cannot do something they can constitutes a useful delaying action while students get ready at the dissertation stage to try again what they were presumably supposed to be able to do when they started. What should they read and how should they read it? Well that depends, just as theorizing does, on what they want to explain. Just as in theorizing, picking too difficult a subject, one not ripe, one beyond current reach, is bound to prove stultifying. Choosing a subject, in plain, is a large part of doing something worthwhile, that is, something interesting yet doable. But reading to choose what to study is not at all the same as reading about how to study what one has already chosen.

Scanning

Selection is all. Knowing what to leave out in reading is almost as important as knowing what to put in. And the two—elimination as well as inclusion—are related. The usual problem is not lack of data or reading material but of inundation and overload. Using additions or modifications to one's body of propositions as the principle of selection depends on developing such a body of lore to begin with. Afraid to start, one never finishes. More fearful of erring by omission, fearful of hearing that one has left something out, one commits the worse sin of overinclusion so that, in the end one does not know what one has learned, feeling always the dread of incompletion. It is better, I say, to err by omission. But how does one decide what to leave out when the purpose is not to absorb an existing body of knowledge, which is problematic enough, but to determine where one's interests lie? Before pursuing a research topic, one must fix on it. Undecided, the potential range of reading is immense, virtually unlimited.

Recall that the point of reading rapidly is to read slowly, to locate the much smaller literature in which to invest oneself. Scanning is a term that seems to fit reading to figure out what to read. Hardly reading at all, except that one does read, scanning properly suggests reading across the tops, skimming really, except that skimming, while near the mark, might be a bit too intense.

Since scanning is a craft skill that cannot exactly be taught but can be learned only by practice, I will have to content myself with some approximate description. Scanning is jumping around. One examines titles or abstracts, alighting on those that appear intriguing without necessarily being able to say why. Trust your intuition. Read the opening lines, the ending lines, a summary if provided, titles of tables, a paragraph here and there. If a spark strikes, read further; if not, go on.

Scanning depends on thinking. Thinking depends on having something to think about. Presumably one has learned a literature. Its propositions are on paper and to some extent in the mind. Go back to them; play with them. It is the interaction between these necessarily inchoate half-thoughts and new material that scanning seeks to evoke. Perhaps someone has placed the usual variables in a different order or defined or measured them in a different way or introduced a new variable or even a new explanation. Perhaps there are different descriptions that, together with what is already active in the brain, bring out hitherto unseen connections. Once that happens a half-thought grows to a two-thirds thought, and one is on his way. Maybe.

Recently I was looking for ways of making the battles of the budget for the last seven years speak to larger questions of political change. Looking through my general file, where I keep things that might be of interest, I came across several that deal with what are called theories of the state. Skimming through them showed me that the authors, mostly Marxists, considered taxing and spending to be important areas of evidence. Apparently the older thesis of the state (an ambiguously enlarged notion of government) as a mechanism of capitalist class rule pure and simple was giving way to debates about the relative autonomy of the state. Perusing footnotes and asking around brought me a couple of books summarizing what their authors called neo-Marxist theories of the state. I scanned them in search of trends. Old concepts from my youth as an aspiring Soviet specialist floated to the surface—the investment strike, false consciousness, total contradictions. But what was this theory that excited scholars beyond the ranks of Marxists? A dual problem for these authors, I gradually came to understand, was how to reconcile their vision with (1) evidence of divisions among capitalist corporations; (2) state action that appeared contrary to their immediate economic interests, such as large welfare programs; and consequent on 1 and 2, (3) the survival of capitalism. In Claus Offe's work, I found a sophisticated state whose officials regulated capitalists better than they could. Flipping back over the reading I had accumulated, I began to see that for these writers the state apparatus under capitalism was playing a similar role to that of the Communist party under socialism. This capitalist vanguard state was the most socially conscious and advanced elements of the bourgeoisie. Just as the Communist party knew workers' interests better than they did, so did the capitalist state know what was good for its adherents. In this way state actions that appeared adverse to corporations could be explained as being in their long-run rather than their short-run interests. Did I have this theory right? I now started to read this literature more closely and of necessity more slowly to find out.

For present purposes it is the sequence of reading that is of interest. First scanning, then skimming, followed by writing, and only then reading. Close reading comes at the end, not at the beginning of a search for a significant subject.

Diverse Purposes

Among the diverse purposes of reading, I begin with learning a field by getting to know what is known. The scope matters. Learning about Congress is less taxing than trying to understand different types of legislatures. Even with so apparently limited and fixed (albeit changing) a subject like Congress, the question immediately arises as to what one wishes to know about it. Every time one scratches the question of purpose, it itches further back, asking essentially, "What is the more specific purpose behind the more general purpose?" Is the purpose of studying Congress to understand how it makes laws or how representatives relate to constituents or interest groups or how a legislature operates under the separation of powers or how any exceedingly fragmented body can make choices at all or why the national debt is so large? What is a poor reader to do?

The first step toward sanity is understanding that reading always has at least a dual purpose: learning about what questions one ought to ask while learning about how existing questions are answered. This means taking two sets of notes, the longer and easier and the shorter and harder. It is easy to become lost in writing down answers, but it is harder (and ultimately more important) to write up questions. For the kind of answers one gets depend on the kind of questions one asks. When readers are able to classify the questions asked and then relate answers to questions, when they also get a glimmer of questions that might exist but have not yet been asked, they are far along.

Learning a field usually involves filling in an already occupied space. Mapping a field, sketching in the contours of open spaces, involve more intellectual effort (as compared to note taking) but has a larger payoff. For the larger the ratio of thinking to reading, the better sense one is able to make of what one has read. Unless the objective is to cover a certain amount of material in a given time, rather than to increase understanding, reducing not expanding the data is required. Another term for this data reduction process is theorizing.

Having arrayed the questions asked about the subject of study, the next step is to review notes and underlining in order to write as concise an account as possible. How are causes related to consequences? What if anything do these consequences cause? The literature helps the reader identify a number of behavior regularities. Explaining why these occur and assessing their consequences in the shortest compass is the purpose of learning a field. When one identifies those readings, or the paragaphs in them, that contribute most to performing this task, the time has come to read more slowly.

At this stage the question of how much to read is readily resolved. At the outset I recommend reading just enough to write a preliminary account of causes and consequences. Then read some more (follow up footnotes, ask others, read reviews, try a recent book or two) and amend (expand or contract) your account. When you run into increasingly diminishing returns, stop. I cannot recall a subfield of study, other than a new language or extensive history, that takes more than six weeks to three months to master.

Reading for Writing

Reading preparatory to writing is (or should be) an extraordinary experience. There is nothing like it. By this time one has mastered a body of literature, chosen a topic, decided what is relevant, fixed on a course of action. Here the concept of moving swiftly to proceed slowly takes on meaning. One cuts a swath through the accumulated literature. Most of it, by far the largest part, is extraneous. No need to give but the merest glance to know that this is not wanted. One zeroes in on the kernel of relevance, those paragraphs, sentences, occasionally phrases, that fit into a preordained scheme. There is a feeling of ruthless precision; everything superfluous is cut away; everything essential is trimmed and shaped, ready to be used as is. Latency is past; maturity is here.

As writing proceeds, reading grows ever more selective. Subtly but surely one's selection criteria change. Being "in the ball park," having the right sort of content, gives way to "Does it fit?" and that in turn to "Will I use this?" From section to section, a secondary criterion emerges: to have nothing left over.

Creativity grows. As the written material substitutes itself for the subject studied, a much smaller number of concepts becomes available for thought. The less there is to think about, the more thought per concept becomes possible. Slow down, one tells oneself, this is getting interesting.

There is elation at discovery. New relationships appear as one manipulates in one's mind the underlying structure. Then a letdown occurs: New relationships require further reading.

Take heart. For as one goes back over this previously recalcitrant material, something special occurs: One's facility has grown; without quite realizing it, one has achieved sufficient mastery to be able to pick out what is wanted. Just as the thought of destruction is said wonderfully to concentrate the mind, the act of writing—putting it down, relating the parts to the whole, investing oneself in the work, making it a part of one— necessarily a highly selective process, teaches one what to look for.

Reading for Pain and for Pleasure

The cliché has it right—everyone has to pay his dues. Nowhere is this more true than in reading for research. Much of it is excruciatingly dull, and by far the largest part will turn out to have been wasted. Absent perfect foresight, knowing at the beginning and in the middle what one can hope to glimpse only at the end—the shape of the completed work—there is nothing to do but to slog through. For the way to the pleasure (no pain, no gain, as body conditioners say) is through the pain.

There is an aesthetic pleasure to be gained from craftsmanship. Out of all this mucking about can (I do not say *must*) come satisfaction at giving shape to this all too recalcitrant material. Even from a numbing routine— counting, sorting, stacking—can come a flow whose rhythm constitutes an innate satisfaction. Take it where you can get it, I say.

There are those for whom the pleasure comes in the reading and the pain in the writing. Bernard Berenson, the self-made arbiter of artistic taste, was one of these. Apparently he was thrown into rages while writing his books. Perhaps the act of composition was too exhausting, weakening the ways he otherwise kept himself together. Any writer can appreciate (though he would not wish to emulate) that feeling of being depleted. Perhaps committing oneself to paper, exposing one's faults to public view, was threatening to Berenson. After all practically everyone else's failures are private. Perhaps the inability to convey on a limited canvass of words the full panoply of observation, to get the subject, if not exactly right, then precisely felt, leads to a sadness that cannot be overcome. Who among us has not felt a sense of betrayal at the unbridgeable gulf between the seemingly splendid vision and the paltry realization.

Making up for Aesthetic Loss

Among the many costs of focusing so narrowly when reading for writing is a loss of the aesthetic whole. One reads snippets, mostly, chapters, occasionally, entire books rarely if at all. This is a serious loss because it is the sense of symmetry and wholeness that one is trying to achieve in one's own work. Yet this loss cannot be made up entirely without sacrificing the benefits, which I have been arguing are substantial, of reading with a purpose.

The one suggestion I have for mitigating this sense of loss comes after a manuscript has been drafted but before it has been published. Increasingly of late I take the time to read neither quickly nor slowly but flowingly and consecutively the book or two related to the research that seem to me best to have realized and gone beyond my own aspirations.

Now I have finished (with Richard Ellis) a draft of a book on *Political Dilemmas of Early American Presidents*. During the research we read remarkable articles by Barry Schwartz on how heroic status was conferred on George Washington, not so much for what he did as general and president but for the fact that he willingly left these offices. In my opinion Schwartz's book, *George Washington: The Making of an American Symbol*, is a triumph of social science. During the research I also reread parts of James Sterling Young's *The Washington Community 1800–1820*, which is about Jefferson's beind-the-scenes leadership that stood in such sharp contrast to his humble-servant public posture. Reading these superbly crafted and extraordinarily well-realized books has buoyed my spirits with a sense of how art and science can come together.

Of course there are always disheartening moments. Penning these words while giving lectures in Leiden, I think the weather here, more changeable minute by minute than anywhere I have been, mirrors the swings in the mood of reading for research. Nothing is so likely to fill one with dismay as the prospect of rereading one's own writing. Yet rereading is also a form of reading and it deserves attention.

Rereading Writing

I know of no better way of improving writing than continuous revision. The problem is falling in love with one's own words. Partial solutions lie in allowing time to elapse, soliciting other people's comments, encouraging collaborators to make changes, working with an editor, and trying to maintain a self-critical attitude. Easier said than done, especially if one has a distinctive style, not readily altered. Now I want to say something about the art of reading one's own work.

First readings are easier than later efforts. At the outset there are obvious errors and infelicities to correct. Omissions quickly become evident. Here word processing helps because it is so easy to make corrections and emerge with a clean copy. But there is also a difficulty; clean pages look like finished copy, especially if printed elegantly.[5] That unjustified feeling should be resisted by going immediately into a second revision. This time one should catch the remaining bloopers.

With the easy-to-spot errors eliminated or diminished, the time comes to look for lapses in logic, coherence, and connectedness. Thus a third review should be more painstaking. Examining connectedness requires looking at the relationship between sections as well as from one paragraph to another. Move paragraphs or sections around, alter old or insert new connecting sentences. I like to do this the third time.

The fourth revision in my sequence (any order one is comfortable with is all right) looks within paragraphs. The ancient verities still apply. Lead sentences should introduce a theme, middle sentences expound it, and the final sentences conclude that thought while preparing the way for the next.

For the fifth revision, a clean copy is helpful because one does not want to be distracted by deletions and additions. Spotting flaws in logic in the internal coherence of the argument must be difficult or one would not have made the mistake in the first place.

By this time one is heartily sick of the whole affair. Nerving up oneself for yet another revision takes an act of will. Do it because it is time to bring in the intended audience. Will those one would want to read this work be able to follow it? Has the necessary groundwork been laid? Is one telling prospective readers too much or too little? Will this article or book get across its message the way it is?

No matter how often one gets this far successfully, there are times when a decision should be made to stop right there and try again another way. Not long ago for instance, I began a new version of *The Politics of the*

Budgetary Process (to be called *The NEW Politics. . .*). I was a hundred or so pages into it when another reading gave me pause. Placing myself as best I could in the position of a layman coming to this subject for the first time, I began to wonder and then to doubt whether my intended reader could follow the account, clear enough for me or other budget aficionados, with the kind of understanding I wanted. After some soul searching (and not a little reluctance), I abandoned the approach I had taken and, alas, along with it buried these pages because they would not fit the new conception. What happened?

Impressed by the radical changes in contemporary budgeting, wishing therefore to give students of the subject the picture as soon as possible, I had begun with a description of the way things are nowadays. It turned out however, or so I began to realize, that the deeper comprehension of the present I sought to convey depended on knowing a lot about the past. That comparison was crucial. The clue was that in revision, I kept introducing paragraphs, then sections about the way it once was. Consequently the manuscript became more and more convoluted, cluttered as it were by so many interruptions. Something had gone radically wrong.

For one, practically everything there that once was in U.S. federal budgeting is still with us; the new typically has been layered onto the old. For another, the old *politics* had been about increments because the base had been mostly accepted; the *new politics* was about the base because it was no longer acceptable. Explaining the present without the past was not informative when it was exactly this change I wanted to explain. Nothing to do then but to adopt a historical mode of exposition. And that worked for me.

But would it work for my other audience, the cadre of informed practitioners and scholars who might be put off by reading so much of what they already knew? I decided that there was so much new in both practice and *The New Politics* that I should take the chance. If I have erred in placing one audience over another, I will surely hear about it.

Try as I might, there was one thing—transport myself in Star Trek time-warp fashion to the days when I was close enough to being a student to know how to write for that audience—I could not do alone. So I sought (and was fortunate to find) a graduate student, Dean Hammer, heretofore innocent of budgetary lore, who served as my student reader. By writing so he could understand (and if not, he told me otherwise), I hoped to come closer to the lay readers for whom *The New Politics* was intended.

Obviously I am not the one to urge on others standards of perfection in which I do not believe and to which I do not adhere. Rules of the kind I have tried to provide (and others only the individual involved can supply) are essential for progress in any endeavor, not only in research. I cannot say how far to carry revision except far enough and not too far. When one begins to wonder whether the latest revisions have made the piece worse, it is time to stop. Whether one is reading to write or writing to read, or as is usual, both, reading with a purpose makes all the difference.

Notes

1. Allan Newell, "Heuristic Programming," in J. Aaronofsky, ed., *Publications in Operations Research*, no. 16 (New York: Wiley, 1969).
2. Ronald Heiner, "The Origin of Predictable Behavior," *American Economic Review* 13, no. 4 (September 1983): 560–95.
3. *The Science of the Artificial* (Cambridge, Mass.: MIT Press, 1969), pp. 90–92.
4. (New York: Free Press, 1963).
5. "You assume," Irving Louis Horowitz wrote me, "that such a technology leads to a confusion between clean copy and finished pages. I suspect that might be true for some scholars. But increasingly, word processing has the reverse effect: making one painfully aware that a work can always be improved upon and revised."

Part II
RESEARCH

4

The Organization of Time in Scholarly Activities Carried Out under American Conditions in Resource-Rich Research Universities

The qualifications in this overly long title are meant to indicate that the conditions under which I work, and on which my suggestions are based, are by no means universal. By American conditions I primarily mean sets of circumstances, some making scholarship easier and others making it more difficult. The U.S. professors who are expected to carry on original research are also (with few exceptions) required to teach. I like and value this arrangement, but like it or not, it affects the time that can be devoted to research. Time devoted to teaching and advising students and preparing lectures cannot be devoted directly to research, though it can, by broadening horizons, extend the scope of the scholar's interests and his familiarity with certain material. When teaching requirements are especially heavy, they may not leave much time and energy for research. American conditions also signify that there is a cadre of professors of relatively equal status rather than, as in Europe, usually a single professor who is also head of a department and personally controls whatever resources are available. European professors may continuously be burdened with administrative duties, but they may also be able to set their own schedules, use junior colleagues and students as research assistants, and have first crack at external research funds. Junior members may have to take what they can get, which may not be much.

The U.S. professors by and large are enmeshed in a tradition of faculty self-government. This, too, I find laudatory. Great universities are characteristically "bottom heavy," for it is in the disciplines and the subdisciplines that most knowledge lies. The price of liberty nevertheless is committee meetings, which can use up much time. The recent proliferation of regulatory requirements, committees on human subjects, reporting on financial interests, and the like, add to the administrative burden—one that is unlikely to be borne to the same degree by European colleagues.

Finally U.S. conditions signify that academics are supposed to carry on research of scholarly merit as judged by their peers and not by external political or bureaucratic forces. This does not mean that professors must stay out of party or policy politics (I do not) nor that they do not engage in advocacy (I do). Rather it means that in addition to whatever else they do, they also write scholarly work and are judged according to criteria internal to their disciplines. Time would be used quite differently if party rallies and pamphlets counted as scholarship or if representatives of external forces or their criteria were used in hiring and promoting (or failing to promote) professors.

By rich research universities, I point to those institutions where research is an acknowledged central priority and that therefore provide the resources necessary to carry it on—a modest teaching load, a decent office, an excellent library, computing facilities, and more. Professors at wealthy universities are also given or have reasonable opportunity to secure such services as secretarial help, speaking to colleagues on the phone, mailing letters and draft manuscripts, even sending material express so a professor can catch up with his mail while on the road. There is no sense advising this exact course of action for scholars in departments that habitually run out of stamps.

Nonetheless the most important resource by far—the uses of the self—are available to everyone. Of course if we think of ourselves as objects out of control—look at poor Aaron, he is so fixed in his ways he cannot change his self-destructive behavior—there is no hope for improvement. But if we are reasonably adaptable, recognizing that we are the most important instrument we will ever possess, then progress is possible. Not a word will be said here about creativity. I do not know more about it than anyone else and that is damn little. Whatever we have or do not have, this chapter is about making effective use of the time we have to do whatever creative work we have in us.

The other side of the coin is that professors in research universities both seek and are obliged to maintain a wide range of external contacts—professional associations; other scholars, domestic and foreign; governmental agencies, private foundations, media of information; and a lot more. A professor who does not do at least some of this (many do all) finds himself out of touch and his students disadvantaged in finding employment and obtaining research funds. For students need not only references for their first job but help throughout their careers for promotion, research grants, and the rest. The professor who stops doing research hurts his former students, just as their accomplishments add luster to his own.

I run a small employment agency out of my office. I read manuscripts for students, colleagues, publishers, and journals. I serve on departmental and campus committees, professional association study groups, and give and listen to lectures in different parts of the world. I answer questions from the media, testify as an expert witness, and speak to alumni. All of these activities are essential, honorable, and a snare. They involve dissipation of effort and fragmentation of time. They are distracting. They are misleading because they suggest one has arrived somewhere when in fact one is only in perpetual transit. The law of the equalization of talent is inexorable: Having done something some people somewhere consider worthwhile, one is invited to travel to talk about it so often that one becomes increasingly less worth inviting.

Yet it would be wrong, in my opinion, to avoid these duties-cum-obligations-cum-pleasures-cum-chores. If one does not review books or articles for scholarly journals, yet expects others to review his, they must do more than their share. Since one benefits from the excellence of his campus and would object if decisions were taken that one did not like, campus and departmental search and policy committees are a must.[1] Honored to be a fellow of this or that, it is only right to return a bit of service. Colleagues and people one does not know personally feel that one's visibility gives them a call on one's time—to answer a question, give a talk, read a manuscript, advise on recruitment, or just show that one recognizes their existence. Not many of these things are terribly time consuming. Some may be evaded or postponed (since I cannot bear long meetings, for instance, I attend far fewer conferences than other people in my position). All in all however, professional time is whittled away bit by bit in an onslaught so varied and inexhaustible—partly brought on by responses to one's own work, partly by changing societal demands, partly by desire to be recognized, even flattered—that it is well nigh irresistible. These demands multiply so quickly that, even as one learns to deflect them, turning down a much larger proportion still leaves an absolutely larger number.

The situation has become so bad that I hear more and more of colleagues who feel they cannot do concentrated research on their home campus. Increasingly therefore they work at home (a practice made easier by interactive word processors, so one can communicate with collaborators without going to campus) or take frequent leaves abroad or even teach at other institutions where they are not responsible for, or responsive to, students, administrators, and others who take up their time.

I have presented this broad-brush version of conditions everyone knows but does not usually talk about because I believe both that they are destructive of scholarly life but can be successfully combated, provided one pays serious attention to the organization of scholarly work. Organization of time is essential if only because the natural forces are all working in the opposite direction.

Honor the Sabbath. Aside from its other benefits, the Sabbath, the inviolable day off, is a protection against the self-absorption that itself becomes a form of fanaticism. The Bible says that the good farmer harvests almost all of his produce, but if some is left in the field, he should not go back for it. This advice is a warning against monomania. Trying to get it all becomes self-worship. The same warning applies to the personal relationships that sustain the scholar in us. These relationships constitute the emotional order on which creative work is built. Our objective is to combine scholarship with life, work with love, not to subordinate the one to the others.

Principles of Self-Organization

The platitudes that follow would not be worth mentioning were they not followed so seldomly. Imposing oneself on the immediate environment, as opposed to being imposed on by it, appears from my observation to be the exception rather than the rule. Perhaps "going with the flow" seems easier, though I will show it certainly is not more effective. Perhaps it appears too difficult or even wrong to deflect or rearrange the tide of interruptions that riddle the day, seemingly making it impossible to engage in sustained effort. Some days it is impossible, at least for me. Even then, as the following principles indicate, I try to be efficient in discharging my duties so there will be marginally fewer interruptions in the future. The problem is how to carve out of most working days a sufficient number of consecutive working hours to make progress in scholarly work.

The principles I am about to enunciate may appear to be (because they are) self-serving. They are designed to help those who employ them. But they are not designed to cheat family, students, colleagues, departments, universities, professions, and governments out of what is their due. Obligations to others, I think, come first, or better still, come with service to oneself. Surely a professor is better able to assist his students (in guiding their work, finding them jobs, dedicating them to scholarship) if he is active professionally. His recommendations and reading of their papers must be more valuable to them if he has done more valuable work. Even when research should be halted to serve others, however, self-organization will see to it that these aspects of one's job are performed in a self-sustaining manner, that is, given their due but not allowed to destroy the individual qualities that make these services worth giving and receiving. Much of what we do is a product of habit, what we do not do, a result of disuse. Whether we want sufficiently to mobilize the self to overcome inertia in the service of higher purposes is the question.

If you are your most important resource, your time is your most valuable asset. Do not fritter it away: Use it.

1. *Do not do anything for yourself others can do for you* (professionally speaking, of course). Do not go to the library unless you want to browse in the stacks. Everything else can be done by assistants (it is especially desirable if your department or research center establishes a library courier service). Libraries are good to use but not to visit. Do not make your own phone calls; do not type your own letters and manuscripts; do not make your own travel reservations. On the contrary, go systematically through your own professional activities and find other people to do them. Of course every principle can be corrupted and has its exceptions. Academics should not delegate meetings with students or colleagues or contributions to faculty self-government. But I do not consider doing my own photocopying part of what I owe the world. There are times when doing things oneself may be more efficacious or just more fun. Call other people yourself if you like doing that and print out your writing on a word processor, especially if you are traveling. But check to see whether the time and effort (typing uses up energy) is worthwhile. The objective is to leave yourself with as much time and energy as you can mobilize.

2. *Spend money* (even, gasp, your own) *to buy time*. Secretarial support and research assistance are (or can be) invaluable. Buying books and photocopying articles instead of borrowing them save me time.

3. *Play when you play, but work when you work*. The incessant interruptions to which academics are subjected appears to have bred in many of us an aversion to continuous labor. Interruptions mean holes in the day, an hour here, a half-hour there. Do not let that time go by unused. Write letters, make phone calls, read and comment on manuscripts for students, colleagues, and publishers. By filling up fragments of your time with things you either must do or want to do, you help preserve time for research.

One way of keeping working time clear is to use lunches to speak to people. I see visitors, do committee business, seek out discussions on scholarly matters, interview job applicants, and speak to friends over lunch. When out of lunch time, I meet people at the end of the day in the faculty club bar. By keeping mornings inviolate, and by expanding afternoons upward through lunches and downward through palaver, I defend my work time.

A few of my friends do things differently; they use their lunches to go swimming (in heated pools, to be sure) or running or otherwise exercise. More power to them! They may well last longer and think more clearly than those who put themselves on the lunch circuit. As should now be clear, there is no one right use of time but numerous ways that contribute differentially to our life and work.

4. *Make interruptions your main business; do not fight them, attend to them.* Devote yourself to students, committees, class preparation, and the rest. Treat them as the most important thing you have to do. And do these things continuously until, for the time being, they are done. It is amazing how much of these nonresearch-related activities can be done when they are all one sets out to do.

In my experience an occasional afternoon, day, or week clears up what appears to be an overwhelming backlog. If a strong and consistent effort does not enable you to find time to sustain research, then shedding obligations is in order, a painful but necessary subject to which I will return.

5. *Organize the flow of work.* Of all subjects to which academics attend, we are weakest, I think, in organizing the flow of our work. The main reason is straightforward enough: We do not think our work has to be organized. After all organization suggests production lines, while we are unique individuals. Consequently we sit around an awful lot waiting for materials we need. Of all the wasted time (telling yourself you are working when you are only being aimless), waiting to work, I think, accounts for the most.

6. *Avoid "downtime."* Think of what you are doing not only in terms of ideas but in terms of organization. What will you need, when will you need it, and how can you get it in time? How far ahead should you plan? About as long (from days to months to a year or two) as it will take *(a)* to get what you want and *(b)* to use what you have. It is necessary therefore to keep in mind (I write them down on a sheet of paper) the research projects you are now doing and would like to do in the foreseeable future. Such planning can be self-defeating if it is too detailed or too rigid. Obviously life overtakes all plans, so they need constant updating. Only in this way, however, can you determine when you will need the requisite material.

I have not yet stated exactly what kind of preparatory material I have in mind. An easy but essential mode of preparation is to keep subject matter files into which you put articles, notes, bibliography, everything at hand that might be relevant. Then when the time comes, you have a head start by marching through this previously prepared material. A file is more useful if you have first read all or part of the material, underlined it, made notes, and sent for new sources from the footnotes. You will then have a wide range of material that is fairly up to date.

General readings are one thing and material relevant to specific chapters is another. To get this far, you must have some idea of where a book or an article is going. Some years ago for instance, I realized that *The Politics of the Budgetary Process* was out of date. Life had changed it from a book about a majority of the budget, namely, domestic appropriations, to a book about a minority of the budget, that is, nondefense discretionary spending. Nor was there literature comparing the major spending programs—social welfare entitlements. Over a number of years therefore, I taught seminars in which students wrote papers about individual entitlements. Then when the time came to write a new book on the subject, I had a base from which to begin.

I do not recommend starting one project immediately on finishing another. Let a little time elapse. Nurture the home front. Take care of other obligations. Go on vacation. Since a lot of energy is required to begin something new, recharging your batteries keeps the instrument in good working order. But always, except when on vacation, think about the flow of work. I like to do that while walking; you can do it while sitting or standing or running. The important thing is that by regarding your time as your most valuable resource, you begin to think seriously about how best to use it.

It is not only what we do but when we do it that increases our efficiency. Many times I have rearranged the order in which I do things to make better use of my time. These matters are entirely situational, hence mundane, but nevertheless important. If I do X first and Y second, instead of the other way around, my secretary will have time to get Z ready, whereas I would otherwise have to wait. If I prepare drafts for a collaborator by a certain time, she will get a revised version to me when I will have time to work on it. A certain paper can be fitted into the time now available, while another paper would be left suspended in midair. By the time I got back to it, I might have changed my mind; in any event I would have to reacquaint myself with the materials, which wastes time.

This approach involves fitting several streams of activities together: commitments to others and to yourself. Your schedule of teaching, committees, lectures, and travel form one stream; another is comprised of your secretary, research assistants, and collaborators. Research requirements, such as interviews and access to special collections that may be located in distant places, form still another stream. Our objective is to merge these streams so they are mutually supportive. Equilibrium is difficult to achieve. Simultaneous equations with numerous variables are difficult to solve. Fortunately a simpler technique is available.

7. *Keep yourself supplied with work.* Start anywhere. If there are no bottlenecks, keep going; if there are, reconfigure until you are kept supplied with work. Suppose you finish a project later or, more rarely, earlier than you had counted on; stretch out the old work to do better or add on new work to get a head start. At every natural stopping point, think again. Before you can go with the flow, it has to flow in your direction.

8. *Do not let the schedule control you; control it.* Is this a counsel of perfection? I think not. Obviously there are commitments with dates attached that have to be met. But you do not have to accept them, at least not entirely. Consider especially the unheard-of alternative of fulfilling them earlier rather than later. Reading a manuscript, writing a letter of recommendation, preparing a lecture, or composing a paper takes the same time whether you do it earlier or later. My practice is to take all small commitments that I know about for six months or a year ahead and fulfill them seriatem before undertaking any larger obligation. This way you avoid a demoralizing overload that becomes so large you have trouble imagining how you will ever crawl out from under it. Steady application overcomes all obstacles, and then you free yourself for the long stretches of time necessary to undertake larger tasks.

9. *Have a rule to have rules.* People respect people who have rules. What is better, others are likely to accept being turned down if it is not personal but is rather part of a system of presumably impersonal rules. A home rule: We (my wife and I) do not buy anything over the phone; please write. Office rule: I do not make decisions about contributing papers or attending conferences over the telephone. Howard Becker writes that

> When people ask me to give a talk about X, or write a paper about Y, or participate in a seminar about Z, I respond by telling them (unless I really find it a useful and interesting thing to do) who they can get who can do at least as good or an even better job than I could. I don't tell them how busy I am, or anything like that, I just tell someone better. Since people who call with these things are mainly looking to solve their own problem of filling up a program or a book or whatever, they are almost as happy to get the recommendation as if I had said yes.

> With respect to talking to the press and other popularizers of social science work, I decided many years ago (after a lot of experience being interviewed about the Drug Problem) not to talk to them unless they would guarantee to print the short quote I gave them as is. Since no one will do that, since it's "against our policy," I decline to speak to them, since it's "against my policy" to do it under any other circumstances. I've also explained to the university's PR people that I will not talk to the press so they might as well stop giving reporters my name. This has cut down a lot on phone calls from those sources.[2]

10. A counsel of perfection: *Work backward, decide how much time you wish to devote to travel, conferences, book reviews, and so on, and*

try to ration your acceptances accordingly. It is not easy to say no to constant importuning. It becomes easier to say no however when you have a good idea of what you have to give up when you take on something else. Applying the principle of opportunity costs gives you a fighting chance to live by your considered priorities.

Travel is the worst. Most of what you hear at conferences is not worth listening to. Meeting people is worthwhile, as is learning about what others are doing. In my opinion nevertheless conferencing has become too much of a good thing. Travel is the enemy of work. It knocks you out coming and going. When you return, piles of promises await fulfillment. Recovery takes longer, both from jet lag and work lag, than is anticipated.

Work, like charity, begins at home. There is nothing like weeks and months of steady work in one place to establish and maintain a research rhythm. Try staying home for a year or six months or one month and see. Since travel is both inevitable and (in part) desirable, however, you ought to make the best possible use of it.

Working on Airplanes and in Hotels

A cross-country flight provides five hours of nearly uninterrupted time; a transcontinental flight provides many more hours. Few work days at a college or university make available that many continuous hours. These are not hours to be gotten through, as if this were a survival course, but to be used to get things done.

The worst thing about travel is coming home. For every day away, it appears, a day or half a day's effort is required to clean up on your return. Thanks to modern technology, combined with conscious self-organization, however, it is possible to take the edge off a bleary-eyed, overburdened homecoming. It does require a bit of cash.

In recent years I have had my secretary (11) *send copies of mail and originals of papers and articles* to me along my travel path, especially the day before returning home. Whenever my schedule permits, or on the plane back, I read the correspondence and answer the letters. Either I write a brief reply in longhand or if more is required, dictate a response on a tape recorder. This way I can just hand the material to my secretary when I arrive without sorting or reading it again. The same practice helps with papers and reports. I throw away what I do not want; if I want to keep it, I write where it should be filed or what else should be done with it. Indeed (12) *if you can not think of what to do with an item, throw it away.*

Although hotel rooms are not ideal places for scholarly work, they will do. Reading is no problem. Writing longhand or on a word processer is feasible. This requires a mental set in which you (13) *tell yourself that this is a work day like any other*. Think of how much better you will feel on your return, especially since you will not be overwhelmed, and these inauspicious surroundings may appear friendlier. Clubs (like the Yale Club in New York or the Reform Club in London) are better because they have fine libraries. Still it is not the place but the person that matters.

14. *Get up early enough to put in two hours before your meeting begins and one hour after it ends*. A lot can be done in three hours. Over a year a lot of three-hour days go a long way. Given time in hotels, you can spread out notes, books, and pads. On an airplane that is difficult, so special thought is necessary to write while on airplanes.

15. *Adapt work to working conditions; take along airplane-compatible work*. Besides reading material, bring past writing to correct. Even under awkward conditions—a hot, crowded, noisy plane—editing a paper resting on a firm pad is possible; so is writing a new paper whose ideas and outline are in your head. For instance, because this chapter is based on my own experiences and observations, it has been written in a notebook on several trips. Picked up and put down on a moment's notice, a paper pad is a good companion for a bumpy ride.

Now as trips approach, I (16) *keep a list or a folder of papers and reviews to work on while in hotel rooms or on airplanes*. In hotel rooms you are your own master. The strangeness of the place is mitigated by a newly found control over time. Another paper was begun at a hotel in Uppsala. It was one of the few long Swedish summer weekends with good weather. The hotel staff had been given the weekend off; I had the key to the building. I told my hosts it was not necessary for them to entertain me further. No mail, no phone calls, no visitors. I began the day by taking a two-hour walk and then spent two hours writing, continuing this practice, except for meal times, for three days. To take advantage of such spontaneous opportunities, however, you must be prepared.

When on trips (17) *always take more than you expect to do*. The purpose of this practice is not to provide a morbid reminder of how much you have left undone, but rather to convert obstacles into opportunities. There is the odd chance your work will proceed faster than expected. There is the greater likelihood that planes will be delayed, schedules disrupted. At such times instead of railing at unkind fate, or fuming at airline personnel, I like to have things to do.

Arrangements may break down. On a trip to a foreign country, for instance, my hosts became paralyzed by internal disputes. Fortunately instead of importuning them or otherwise making myself disagreeable to no purpose, I wrote one paper and two book reviews by the time my schedule was reinstated.

Given a choice between planes or trains, I go by train because they provide better places to work. Once at your destination, (18) *act like you are working so you will be left in peace*. There is no certain safeguard against the loquacious and unwanted companion, but a show of being engaged in work will ward off most interruptions. A word in advance about not being disturbed for meals (he who flies for the food is a fool) or movies or headsets or surveys or games goes a long way.

On the way back, a tired person may not feel like working. Fine. Enjoy. But if you do wish to work, try sleeping first and then refreshed, return to work. Do not force it, especially not writing, because the effort will be wasted. When you have gotten into good work habits, you should better be able to forgive yourself for not working when it is inappropriate to do so.

Jet lag grows as you grow older, or so I find. I have found it useful to eat lightly and get into the swing of the place to which you are heading, even if that means pushing a bit to stay up late. Getting up in the morning at the same time as other people helps me. This works going west to east, but nothing much helps on the way back. Well a little suffering may be good for the soul.

Self-Defense

19. *Defend your work time, but having done so, bend a little*. Do not be a workaholic; it is bad for you and for those around you. My aim has not been to tell anyone to work endless hours. Personally, except for some reading, I do not work evenings or weekends.[3] On the contrary, my aim in giving advice has been to make more productive use of fewer hours. In order to accomplish this purpose, however, it is necessary to protect your work time. If you do not, who will?

It does not matter when you work, only that you protect the time you have set aside for work. I do not schedule classes then nor do I go to meetings. I do bend when colleagues or students can find no other time, but I make them show me why I must for, if not, most of my work time would dissipate. Since pressures to invade work time are incessant, vigilance is necessary.

If you cannot stand interruptions, do not make telephone calls during work time. My preference, sitting on the West Coast, is to take calls until and unless they become disruptive. The reason is that calling people back in the afternoon, especially if they are in the East or Europe, is more trouble than the interruptions.

20. *Keep conversations with students businesslike*. Their tendency to wander from classroom or research subjects to their life histories, sports,

or other extraneous matters should be resisted. The same principle applies to publishers' representatives and other visitors. In this way you can provide all the time necessary for meeting your responsibilities without sacrificing interminable amounts of time. A brisk businesslike attitude is also conducive to maintaining and teaching by example a proper professional stance. Leave "the whole person" to priests, rabbis, and lovers.

I am ambivalent about giving advice against working at home. Though I prefer to separate home from office, I cannot say that those who feel besieged in their offices or are psychologically unable to defend their space should not work at home. But there is a collegial cost: The more people who stay home, the fewer interactions between them and their would-be colleagues. Consequently collegial life becomes impoverished, and I would like to hold on to those interactions as long as possible.

One reason professors claim they cannot work at their universities is that they travel so often they cannot maintain a steady pace. Abroad, they are of course less well known, so requests for appearance decline, and they feel they are able to get more done.

Rather than making more frequent trips, those who desire to work at their home bases should try to (21) *group together lectures and conferences*. Aside from traveling less, which reduces wear and tear, such grouping together reduces constant disruption and hence increases continuous work time. And steady effort of course is the secret of accomplishment.

Reading may be the enemy of writing. One way of gaining continuous time is to concentrate on writing, leaving reading in your field, broadly conceived, to another day. Should you follow this strategy? Yes and no. Yes, it is desirable to concentrate on one thing at a time; (21) no, *it is not desirable to stop reading outside of your immediate project.* Plucking the fruit of past labors while failing to fertilize and water the roots from which future creativity comes is shortsighted. (The practice is tantamount to foundations that want credit for financing a scholar's latest project but are unwilling to nurture the institutional base from which future creativity must necessarily flow.)

22. *Cut it short.* Write the shortest possible letters and memorandums and make quick calls. Stick to business. This art can be learned. There is of course a dividing line between being brief and being abrupt, no doubt I err in the latter direction. Many memos do not have to be written at all; a call would do. But if you have to write, get to the essence and stop. Your recipients will appreciate it.

Do write brief notes to people whose articles or books you admire; they seldom get fan mail. My practice is to write first to people from obscure places and small institutions; they are often shunted aside. A long letter is appropriate when the correspondence is personal or scholarly and there are substantive points to be covered. But do not spend time when it is not necessary.

Shedding Obligations

When things get out of control; when we feel it is all too much; when more threatens to leave us with less, how do we shed obligations?

23. *Stop the hemorrhage; do not take on new obligations.* Just as organizations losing cash first try to break even and as doctors seek to stem the flow of blood to preserve the body before restoring it to health, so the first objective is to stop making things worse. Easier said than done. We get into such situations both because we want to do these things (they are individually desirable, only aggregately harmful) and because we feel obligated.

When the smaller tasks threaten the larger ones, it is time to call a halt. Refuse new invitations. It is difficult to resist targets of opportunity, blandishments, recognition, travel, and all the rest. But resist you must; otherwise tasks that ought to be fulfilling, like exploring a new subject, become filled with dread. Life becomes a treadmill. When you start wondering what you ever saw in scholarship, take a new tack. Write what and as you please. If you can fulfill a request with something on hand or that you wanted to do anyway, fine; if not, say no. Hard as this position is to maintain, it produces peace. When you start out, of course, you may be looking for opportunities, and you may not be in a position to refuse requests. But then again you have accumulated fewer obligations.

Teaching diverse courses has the advantages of increasing exposure to a varied subject matter. Continuously developing new courses is another matter. Having just taught a new course, a faculty member has good reason to restrict the rapid introduction of additional new subjects. Maintaining a fixed array of courses for a time is an aid to both learning and stablizing the time devoted to course preparation.

It would appear that by preventing things from getting worse, by limiting the time devoted to other activities, and by working during the remainder, the problem of overload may be managed. Maybe. So far however this has been a purely static analysis. I have assumed that the level of demand remains constant; often it does not. Thus the person who becomes skilled at dealing with a constant level and source of demands soon finds that last year's strategy will not do for this year's difficulties. People who have learned through an evolutionary process to reject 99 percent of the demands on their time discover that when these demands increase several times over they are as far behind as ever. A decision rule that once generated, say, a hundred demands a year now produces two hundred. In a corresponding manner, changes in the sources of demands take time to counter. Perhaps they were national and now have become international; perhaps they were from lower status organizations, and the new ones are higher status; perhaps these units paid less and now pay much more. Alternatively as you learn the importance of turning down well-paid assignments that do not fit in with the development of your work, a new set of demands arises from sources that appeal to other motives—ideological, religious, prideful. All the more reason then, facing a moving target, to get better at using them. For if you become more efficient while demands become more numerous, it may still be possible to do scholarly work while teaching and administering at your home university.

There is a lot of lying. People say it is impossible when they mean undesirable. They pretend to be out of town or otherwise indisposed. Bad acting is everywhere evident. A familiar scene involved a professor of foreign languages with a better command of English than most natives who pretended to speak so badly, with such accented phrases, that students could not understand. This, together with numerous nervous twitchy mannerisms, all put on, and a general air of hopeless incompetence, was sufficient to convince everyone that he could not be trusted to perform the simplest administrative tasks. Very amusing except that others are thereby disadvantaged.

The other side of this treacherous divide is the martyr complex: Look at how I am suffering for my ungrateful colleagues. It is absolutely true that your colleagues do not appreciate the essential administrative duties you performed. It is true as well that after years of being a chairman or admissions officer or graduate or undergraduate adviser or placement officer, the lucky incumbent, on leaving office is likely to be asked what he has written lately. The proper attitude is bemusement at the human condition. It is not true however that the martyr is suffering. Were that so he would have quit long ago.

The Margin Is the Opportunity

Why all this fuss about scraping up little bits of time? Why bother to pick up a few minutes by writing instructions on the disposition of mail and another few minutes by writing short letters? Is this minute squeezing not the sort of monomania I have presumably been arguing against?

Not at all. The bulk of time is necessarily taken up with maintenance—doing things to continue a pattern of life. Teaching, answering mail, committee work, and all that are essential. But they just keep you going. Creative work, progress, new things that take you beyond where you have been, depend on the availability of time to move forward. Thus the future, so to speak, lies in the increment.

It is right that the rest of your life should be larger than your scholarly work. It is wrong that the creative portion—better still, carving out the opportunity for creativity—should be so small. (24) *The incremental illusion denies you the opportunity—analysis of the whole, makes the increment worthwhile, but analysis of the increment by itself wrongly suggests it is worthless.* A decade ago I spent two years in New York City where a car is counterproductive. I told myself that it would be far less expensive and far more convenient to rent on the odd occasion. When that time did arrive however analysis of the incremental costs—Why spend $167 and go through the bother of rental to see cousin Izzy?—led me to stay home. Increments of time only look small when they stand in isolation. Indeed no one increment by itself is worth much in terms of the opportunity to write or do research. Only when they are aggregated does securing each increment add up to something worthwhile.

Another good reason for making (25) *efficient use of time* is that it *makes it easier to let go.* Knowing that you are ordinarily efficient, I find, makes it easier to cope with impossible days. Your parking space is taken, you receive a ticket. The roof leaks and you cannot find the roofing contractor, *X* drops in from out of town, followed by an emergency committee meeting to which key participants are late. What to do? Nothing, absolutely nothing. Laugh if you can. When the student for whom you have read innumerable drafts corrects all his old errors, taking care however to introduce new ones each time an old one is extinguished so you feel your time has been wasted, the memory of better days should carry you through.

Individuation

For those who are dismayed at what they have read, there is also Kahneman's rule: Do not read about rules about what you ought to do but will not follow because they will only make you guilty. Before reading a draft of this chapter, Kahneman told me he rode on airplanes without working and also without guilt; now he does no more but feels worse about it.[4]

Nothing said here is meant to deny the existence of importance of differences among people. Some people work faster or slower, with more or less intensity, to better or worse effect. So be it. To deny individual differences would be like denying life.

I have not sought to substitute for the allocation of talent but to acquire some understanding of how to use our native abilities. Just as I have not suggested working a hundred hours a week, but rather how to make the most out of a 40-to-50-hour week, so my emphasis is on efficiency—getting more desired output from a fixed input—as distinguished from creativity. The point is not that others should do as much (or as little) as I or anyone else does, for that is purely idiosyncratic, but that we should all make good whatever promise is in us. Indeed my message has been that in order to fulfill the promises we make to ourselves and to others, we ought both to make fewer promises and more effective use of ourselves.

Notes

1. A colleague writes that his sense of priorities differs because the local conditions under which he works are different. He serves on department committees because in his institution they matter. He does not serve on campus-wide committees because they do not matter. So be it. I give readers my constants in order to provide a steady source of advice. *Ifs* and *buts* do not belong here. But my constants may also be your variables. Start here, I suggest, without necessarily ending where I do because (*a*) we differ and (*b*) so do the conditions under which we work.
2. Letter from Howard Becker to author, August 3, 1987.
3. There is an exception to this. Most years I work only three- or four-weekend days. Last year (the 1986–87 academic year), I worked about 20-weekend days in order to finish books that had bunched together and (so I tell myself) to make life easier thereafter. We shall see.
4. Conversation with Dan Kahneman before a committee meeting.

5

The Open-Ended, Semistructured Interview: An (Almost) Operational Guide

Dean Hammer
Aaron Wildavsky

When a reporter or historian interviews a source who was a participant in the events being studied, or a social scientist seeks to understand a process by talking to the people involved, the chances are they are using the open-ended, semistructured interview. This type of interview, like most things we wish to define, can be characterized by what it is not as well as (approximately) what it is. Closed interviews have questions that are fixed, if not for all time, then at least for the duration of the project in which these interviews figure. The questions are structured as well in that they are asked and the responses recorded in a given order or a given cycle and in a given way. Neither the content nor the manner of asking the questions is supposed to vary. Ideally allowing for the failure (or the inability of interviewers) to follow their instructions, each interviewer is an interchangeable part, for the purpose is to achieve as high a level of standardization as human ingenuity and malleability will allow.

By contrast in the open-ended interview everything is provisional. Having soaked himself in the subject matter, our intrepid interviewer is free to try out numerous questions to see which will secure the most revealing results. Questions may be abandoned, altered, and tried again. Especially important are follow-up queries, with such creative locutions as why and what else. These questions are semistructured in that there is supposed to be some "method in the madness," some patterns to the questions, some holding on to ones that show promise. The interview is only semistructured (as in semitough) in that the questions and the mode of asking or following them up are intended to vary according to the discretion of the interviewer.

Semi means that one of the aims of this bundle of interviewing techniques is to come up with an approach (questions plus style) that is well suited to the research project at hand. The outcomes are also semigood in that they can be only imperfectly achieved. Understanding this much—that you can do better but must always fall short—is part of both the armory and the armor of the would-be open-ended, semistructured interviewer. It helps to understand why the interviewer's performance necessarily falls short of his promise.

Given the nature of the beast, the open-ended, semistructured interview cannot be done perfectly. The best that can be expected is not too bad or better still, not so bad as before. Good advice can be given, but it cannot be followed exactly as given. The reason is that the usual prescriptions, including our own, tend to be proverbial (that is, mutually contradictory—many hands are better than one but too many cooks spoil the broth). Circumstances, as lawyers say, do alter cases. And these circumstances are so numerous and varied, including the personalities of the interviewer and the respondent, the conditions of the time and the organizations involved, the sensitivity of the subject, and much more, some of which involves subtle matters of social interactions, that no one can claim to understand but a small proportion of them. The first requirement for those who wish to accept this daunting task without self-destructing is *courage*. The second is *resilience,* the capacity to bound back, to learn from error how to do a bit better, to be buffered from adversity—rejections, hostility, missed opportunities—and go at it again. The third and final requirement is *self-management,* the use of personal experience to develop a personal style of interviewing that will withstand the blows and bridge the gaps and inconsistencies in the prescriptions that follow. There is fun, too. Even pleasure and an aesthetic sense of hitting the right chord are possible. But first you must have courage, resilience, and self-management.

The kind of interviewing we are discussing is a product of social interaction taking place under severe time constraints, unequal status, and decidedly mixed motives. Looking good to the relevant other is a human preoccupation that does not distinguish between interviewer and interviewee. However the person being interviewed has much more practice in managing the impressions he gives than you do in digging beneath the surface. It is an unequal contest. The best you can do is to even up the contest a bit. But even when you have succeeded in knowing more about certain aspects of his office than he does (after all he does not have the time or the right to ask everyone else what they are up to nor the hope of getting honest answers), you cannot let him know that you know, otherwise you risk becoming one of those mythical victims of 1930 gangster movies, who, as he disappeared into a watery grave in cement shoes, was dispatched with the words no scholar could ever mutter: "He knew too much." Actually it is advantageous to let on you know some things because trading inside news may be good for the interview. Then again revealing confidences is not done (1) because it is dishonorable and (2) because it is counterproductive—word will get out that you are untrustworthy and no one will speak to you again.

All respondents appear to be busier than any interviewer. All the interviewer has to do, or so it seems, is interview, while the person being interviewed is doing his job, a job full of interruptions (at crucial moments). If you cut short the interview (to gain good will or simply to show human kindness), you may never get back in again due to illness, transfers, lawsuits, and other unfortunate happenings. If you push your luck, annoyance may leave you, the bedraggled interviewer, not only without vital answers but without hope of ever getting them. What to do?

Nothing, really, except perseverence. You place your bets and take your chances. There are often things to try, but rarely superior alternatives (until afterward when it is too late). And that is exactly the point we have been trying to make.

Because it involves the vagaries of human nature, multiplied by social interaction—i.e., diverse natures, with semi-opposing interests and incentives, hurriedly done amidst mounting time pressures, with neither party quite certain of what they want to give and get—interviewing without much structure or closure is an extremely uncertain business. Ambivalence is its middle name. That is its joy and its disappointment. That is why creativity that cannot be pre-programmed is called for.

That is also why specific advice is called for—to cut through the ambiguity—and is bound to be faulty—because no specific move can cover over the inherent uncertainties of brief, asymmetrical, mixed-motive encounters.

The prescriptions that follow for devising, conducting, and writing up open-ended, semi-structured interviews were compiled from two uneven sources: the written literature (as compiled by Dean Hammer) and Aaron Wildavsky's efforts to pass on his semi-satisfactory experiences to his students. Footnotes or initials identify the guilty parties. When in doubt, stick with it and make error your friend.

Open-ended interviewing requires the cultivation of a relationship. As in any human relationship, rules are limited in application so that getting the most out of the interview relies largely on judgment that can be developed only through experience. Of course, acquiring this experience means you must survive your first interviews. The rules that follow can be thought of as a survival kit, something to hold onto until you can be guided by your own experience.

Preparing for the Interview

A successful interview begins with thorough advanced preparation. Fundamentally *you need to become (and remain) familiar with the objectives of the interview*. This seems almost too basic to mention, but it is easy to become sidetracked and lose sight of the general goals of the project.[1] The interviewer who wants to find out about the different strategies used by the respondent under various conditions, for instance, should not be diverted by family history or why civil servants receive no respect. Since interviews are interactive and mutual, however, respondents may use them for their personal purposes. The trick here is gently but firmly to bring the respondent back to the desired pattern of questions. The best general advice is to use something, anything, in the response ("Do you attribute your later success in——to this early childhood fixation?") to get back on track. Whose interview is this, anyway.

Sometimes, Lewis Dexter reminds us, sharing a peripheral interest with a respondent leads to a fuller picture of the kind of person being interviewed. Rapport may be enhanced. True. But all this takes time. Only experience (and that is not always reliable) enables the interviewer to sense when going outside the subject will enable him ultimately to enter into it more fully.

A counsel of perfection: Being able to sort out central from peripheral topics will save you and the respondent time. Focus, which is possible when you know what information you want, increases the depth and the concreteness of responses, since you will be able to spend more time and effort concentrating on a special issue. Asking, "So what can you tell me?" about everything is likely to get you nothing.[2] Then again if you already knew what you wanted to ask, you might be using a different type of interview or be near the end instead of the beginning of your project. What is central may be a product of research rather than its prerequisite.

As well as knowing or guessing what data you need, you should also *try to anticipate the responses likely to come from any particular interview*. This requires getting to know about the individual and his job within the organization. Knowing this, you will be in a much better position to steer the discussion toward areas in which the respondent has particular expertise and insight.[3] Too much preconception of course is likely to lead you astray by rendering you less sensitive to what the respondent is trying to communicate. Be familiar but only a little so the respondent can explain the true meaning to the uninitiated. *Anticipate but not overly* is the delicate balance you seek to achieve. Polonius could hardly give better advice.

Becoming familiar with the interviewee's situation (for example, his role in the organization) increases the likelihood that you will be able to explore effectively the implications of particular statements. Equipped with a knowledge of the situation as it appears to be, the interviewer

> can readily distinguish the objective facts of the case from subjective definitions of the situation. He thus becomes alert to the entire field of "selective response." When the interviewer, through his familiarity with the objective situation, is able to recognize symbolic or functional silences, "distortions," avoidances, or blocking, he is the more prepared to explore the implications.[4]

While we are certain that Robert Merton and Patricia Kendall hear through silences and see through distortions, ordinary mortals can only hope to educate their perceptions to recognize invariably selective responses.

Knowledge can also be helpful in stirring the respondent's memory. The better versed you are about the history of the organization and the individual you are interviewing, the greater chance you have of being able to mention some detail or event that will spark the memory of your informant.[5]

Always remember that you, the researcher, are the theorist, not the person you are interviewing. Aside from the fact that action-oriented people are unlikely to be introspective, they are experts on what they did or do and what they perceive. From their responses your task is to build a description and then interpretation of the phenomena you are investigating. *Asking respondents who has the power is wrong; asking them what they did or observed is more like it.*[6]

To aid you in this task, *you should understand the function of the organization.* Do not give the interviewee the impression that you are coming in out of the cold. Ignorance of the association's most rudimentary function is likely to result in wasted time. Beginning the interview with "What does your organization do?" indicates to the respondent that you are not prepared for an informed or technical discussion. The interviewee will likely feel that he must carefully go over the basics with you, taking time away from exploring important issues.[7] Contrarily, as Lewis A. Dexter advises in his seminal study, the respondent is likely to appreciate and be more comfortable with the interviewer who has taken the time to understand, at a basic level, what the organization does.[8] The contrary danger is wrongly believing you have to know too much, which can lead to paralysis. A little knowledge helps.

Lacking knowledge about a subject creates a dilemma for the interviewer: Either you can interrupt the respondent because you do not understand, thereby disrupting the flow of the interview and leaving the impression that you are not prepared to discuss the subject in depth, or you can continue the interview without being sure about what is being said, hoping that everything will become clear later on. In the event that you do come across an area that you do not understand, it is better to clear up the confusing statements before moving on.[9]

Become acquainted, if you can, with the structure of the organization. This means not only understanding its formal hierarchy (thereby enabling you to determine who the subordinates are and who reports to whom) but also its informal social relationships. You should also try to familiarize yourself with the personnel the respondent comes in contact with as well as people whom they do not see.[10] This sort of information on what relationships exist between members of the association will help you determine whom to interview first and what sorts of questions to ask each interviewee. Our permissive "if you can" indicates that such information is useful but not indispensible. If you want to know everything before you start, you will have trouble getting started.

Finally *you should try to investigate the outlook of individuals in the organization.* Different people, depending on their attitudes toward the organization, their feelings toward other workers, or their ego needs, will supply vastly different types and amounts of data. There are several kinds of respondents who are likely to divulge a great deal.

1. The naïve respondent who speaks without thinking about the implications of his statements.
2. The frustrated individual who harbors resentment against the organization because of blocked ambitions.
3. The secure veteran who has little to lose from any statements he might make.
4. The individual in need of ego stroking; this person will try as hard as possible to please the interviewer as long as the interviewer continues to make him feel needed.
5. The subordinate who must always cow-tow to his superiors; this individual may be waiting to tell it all.[11]

Then again resentment does not necessarily lead to clear vision. Quite the contrary. Respondents who will do in their fellows may well be the most unreliable. After all if they will undermine people they know well, why should they hesitate to mislead you? *Attend to the overeager,* our motto is, *but triple check the spiteful and loose tongued.*[12]

The worst sources of all are the people who have talked themselves (and, alas, possibly the researcher as well) into thinking that what others just like them believe is true because the right people believe it. Our next adage, as you might have guessed, is to *double and triple check the reliable as well.*[13]

There are also respondents who are likely to have unique insights into any given area. These would include:

1. The outsider, who sheds the light of a different culture, class, set of experiences, and so forth, on the organization; this might be a recent immigrant who has become involved in politics or the first woman to occupy a position previously dominated by men.
2. The novice whose experiences in the new job are still salient; the novice may be able to reveal practices and attitudes that other more veteran members have taken for granted.[14]

It is even possible, we might add, that people with long experience may have something to say. In fact one of our best tips is to *start interviewing with retired personnel, the older the better.* Time weighs heavily on their hands. They know they once were important, but nobody else does . . . except you. They will give you hours, even days. And they will pave your way to their successors. By the time you reach those who occupy similar positions in the present, you will know a lot that your respondent would like to know. Interviewing is a transaction, a bargain between consenting adults. *Trade what you have learned for what you would like to know.*[15]

Once you have an idea of what information you hope to obtain from the interview, and after you have researched the organization and its members, *prepare a tentative order of topics and subtopics to be covered.* Thinking ahead of time about the topics to be discussed helps to ensure adequate coverage during the interview. You do not want to leave the interview kicking yourself for not having thought to ask several questions. You might not get a second chance to speak to that person.[16]

You may wish to *order the topics to best stimulate an individual's memory.* For topics that require recall of past events, you may wish to ask the questions chronologically, or you may begin with questions that are most easily remembered. Once memory has been stimulated, you can then more easily pursue the difficult questions.[17]

You can also *order questions to stimulate the respondent's interest.* You may for example start with questions of particular concern to the respondent and then move to those of less interest. Or you may want to alternate between exciting and dull subjects. If the respondent is interested in your topic, he is likely to enjoy thinking about the subject and in probing his own memory.[18] After all no one wants to answer boring questions.

In any case you will want to pace the interview by alternating between questions requiring reflective responses and questions that are much easier to answer. You do not want the interview to sound too mechanical, nor do you want to wear out the respondent.[19]

While you should have an idea of what topics you would like to cover (and in what order), this preparation should be only tentative. We will discuss later the many different unexpected occasions that can arise and how you can deal with them. Suffice it to say for now that the good interviewer remains flexible: The ability to adjust to resistant informants or the fortuitous discovery of a wealth of unanticipated data will pay healthy dividends. Staying flexible but firm is another indication of melding opposites, which is the lot of the bemused interviewer.[20]

In conjunction with ordering topics and subtopics, you should *prepare guide questions*. These are simply questions that the interviewer formulates beforehand. Unlike a preplanned questionnaire, though, guide questions should be kept to a minimum.[21] Hence we reformulate in the spirit of this enterprise: *Use guide questions, but only sparingly.*[22]

Use guide questions for potentially touchy subjects. By thinking ahead about possible awkward situations and by working out wording in the calm before the interview, you may be able to avoid the embarrassment of having to search for appropriate phrasing.[23] Well-formulated guide questions can provide a much easier way of introducing delicate subjects than simply "winging it." Which of these situations would you rather be in? "Are you saying you illegally . . . I mean, were illicitly involved in this activity" or "What did you do when?" There will be enough awkward situations so that you will later greatly appreciate any advanced planning.

You may also *use guide questions for important points to ask when lulls occur in the interview*. There will be occasions when a subtopic will be exhausted and a sudden pause arises. Instead of looking at each other uncomfortably, and rather than having the interviewer scramble for any question (even one that is pointless and thus a waste of precious time), guide questions can be a quick reference for smoothly broaching a new topic.[24]

Guide questions reduce interviewer anxiety but also lead to overstructuring the situation. To realize the benefits of the open-ended format, there has to be room for follow-ups. You know yourself better than we do. Use guide questions, we say with conviction, but not too many.

Beginning the Interview with the Right Person

Whom should you see first? Opinions differ. Dexter suggests that your first interviews will most likely be relatively unproductive and that in fact this may be for the good.[25] These initial contacts are warm-ups for the interviewer; they can be useful for getting back in practice, becoming acquainted with information you are likely to encounter in subsequent interviews, and perhaps highlighting some potentially touchy subjects among other participants.

There is the contrary argument that the interviewer should first question higher status individuals and then move down the hierarchy to those working more in the field. Top officials, it is argued, often possess a broad perspective on the happenings of the organization. Thus they are presumably in a better position than people lower down in the organization to understand what the goals of your project are. Consequently these higher status officials may be able to point you in lucrative directions that field workers would not have had sufficient perspective to suggest. Furthermore once the upper echelon has cooperated, those farther down in the hierarchy will feel they have permission to go along with the research.[26]

The disadvantage of starting at the top is that you do not then know enough to make effective use of the interview. The respondent may consequently send word down that you are not worth the time the interview takes. When you do become better informed, if you are allowed to get that far, the top people may refuse to give you more time. A reasonable compromise is to try to gain access to someone at or near the top, reveal your ignorance, explain your project, ask a few questions, cut it short, and ask if you can come back when you know more.[27]

There is more general agreement that you should *start with individuals more favorably disposed to being interviewed.*[28] These informants will likely be more responsive, providing you with a substantial base of knowledge to proceed and not to be underestimated, starting off your interviews on a good foot. The confidence from these initial interviews may well carry you over when respondents turn nasty or the information momentarily dries up.

There are as usual exceptions to this rule. Those who are more favorable to you are likely to share your preconceptions. Consequently "starting out with them may in fact lead the interviewer to rely too much and too long on unchallenged assumptions which would be more quickly questioned through interviews with others." A second concern is that concentrating your attention on a certain type of person may result in the interviewer being labeled as on his side. This demarcation is especially likely in an organization riddled with factions.[29] Here again the retired (as well as those who have jobs elsewhere) provide a good send off. Your interest in them will often be returned by forbearance for your ignorance.

Finding the Perfect Place

The place to meet will set the context for your interaction with the interviewee. Generally speaking *conduct the interview in a professional, private place*. This place is usually the individual's office. That will provide enough privacy so that the person can speak without fear of being over-heard and will also set a professional tone for the interview.[30]

If the respondent may be constantly distracted in his work environment, you should consider interviewing in a more private place. Constant inter-ruptions will destroy the flow of the interview and hamper the concentra-tion of the respondent. Additionally when continually reminded of the needs others have of him, the interviewee may feel some compulsion to get back to work rather than speak to you. Human interruptions need not be the sole culprit here; an individual can be distracted simply by the environment. Think for example about interviewing a teacher in his classroom, surrounded by unread papers to be graded and lesson plans still to be prepared. You will want to avoid those situations where compet-ing time demands on the respondent arise.[31]

You do not want all interruptions to be halted. Letting phone calls come in allows you to see how the individual deals with others (as well as giving you a chance to catch up on your notes).[32] Interviewing on the job also provides you with an opportunity to observe the working environment, including scanning the respondent's desk for memos or documents that may be lying there,[33] observing how the whole office is set up (for example, are doors to offices opened or closed; are desks piled high), and seeing how employees interact with each other (including how the interviewee treats others).[34] The interviewee may also feel more comfortable in his own setting and become tense in unfamiliar or (what is perceived to be) less neutral environments. For example a principal's office would not be the place to interview teenagers about drugs in school.[35]

Where do you go if the private office is unsuitable? Going out for lunch or dinner is not advisable because there is the chance you will be inter-rupted by friends or associates of the respondent. Additionally writing notes and keeping track of what has been said is difficult while eating.[36] A final drawback to taking out a respondent for a meal is the cost. Your project will have finite funding; there are probably better ways to spend your finances than on a situation that may not yield very good results. Contrariwise accepting a free lunch may create a sense of obligation or partiality you wish to avoid. Paying your own way is good for the soul.[37]

Meeting at the respondent's home is a mixed blessing. The advantage of the home is that the respondent will feel fairly comfortable and secure there.[38] The drawback is that the interviewee may allow his family to enter and leave the room, thus inhibiting the flow of the discussion.[39]

There are some alternative interview sites to choose from. Usually the interviewee's workplace will have conference rooms available. This will provide the privacy that might not be available in a busy office. Or you can go for a walk. Often the time outside the office will prove to be a nice break for the respondent. Then again it is not easy to write while walking.[40]

You need to consider what time to meet for the interview. The best rule of thumb is to *ask the respondent when he can best meet*. There may be times when the respondent is less relaxed or more likely to be continuously interrupted by others. Or the respondent may want to choose a time (and place) so that he will not be seen being interviewed, either because he fears repercussions in the office or just feels more comfortable remaining anonymous.[41]

It is not so much that we disagree with this received wisdom, though we do in part, but that it amazingly omits the most important rule of all: *Get the interview anywhere, anytime you can, provided only that the setting is moral and safe.* You are unlikely to be able to set the terms—where, when, how—on which the interview will take place. Take it as it comes, some time being better than none. The respondent can usually be counted on to recognize an impossible situation. If not, a little suffering goes with the territory.[42]

One more thing. Gentlemen (and gentlewomen) do not read other people's mail—or their memos. It is wrong to play the sneak. Besides a reputation for sneaky behavior will certainly ruin your interview and possibly your project.[43]

Making Contact

Most people are quite willing to give interviews.[44] Interviewing may fulfill ego needs of the respondent (the need for recognition, for feeling needed or important);[45] the interview may be cathartic, allowing the informant to get something off his mind;[46] or interviewing may be satisfying because of the psychic need for interaction.[47] The interviewee may wish to contribute to your education or feel a duty to scholarship. Or he may just be polite.[48] You should try to discern the motivations of the respondent (although this will often be difficult). Is the respondent trying to get back at someone, trying to clear his name, or is he just attempting to be helpful to you? Understanding why the interviewee is speaking the way he is can aid you in deciphering his responses.

When you make contact with the respondent, you will need to explain who you are and what your project is about. *Be general about what you are looking for.* Do not go into a great deal of detail about the aims of your project. In all likelihood the respondent is not interested in the detail you are capable of providing. Additionally saying too much risks unintentionally stumbling on a purpose that alienates the interviewee. For example, rather than mentioning to a budgeting official, "My hypothesis is that budgeting is out of control," it is better to state, "I am examining the budgetary process." Speaking in general terms allows the respondent to interpret the scope and aims of the study as he sees fit.[49] Since you do not yet know how your project will come out or exactly what you are looking for, a general description is straightforward enough.[50]

You should provide a truthful explanation of your research. "Bluffing, pretending naiveté, representing oneself or one's sponsors as something misleading, or trying to make one's study appear *more* or *less* important than it actually is are *all* dangerous tactics. Subsequent events or other lines of communication may reveal the real situation to the field contacts and seriously damage the research worker's field relations."[51] Need we add that lying is wrong even if efficient.[52]

Do not explain your project so that is poses a threat to the respondent. If the interviewee believes that he is going to be carefully scrutinized, then he is likely to resist being interviewed (and will certainly be less forthcoming if he does decide to talk with you). Doby, for example, compares these two openings: "We want to study what makes for good and bad union leaders" and preferably, "We want to learn how a union carries on its day-to-day work."[53]

While we agree that you should not threaten the respondent, we object to this formulation on two grounds: (1) There is nothing necessarily threatening about saying that you are studying leadership (except to researchers who can never figure it out). *The interviewer need not be overly pointed,* we should say, but he should not dissemble. (2) The form of the question about leadership suggests that the respondent is being asked to theorize. If respondents were good at it, we would fear unemployment in the academy.

You should present the project in terms that will be of interest to the interviewee. The idea of the opening is to get the respondent to support your project. For example you might approach the topic you are doing in this way: "You have probably read and heard about some of the problems of youth in our city. We are interested in talking with parents about the difficulties of raising children these days."[54] Such an opening provides a clear appeal to the expertise of the parent and suggests a need by the interviewer for the parent's input.

If asked about who is sponsoring your project, emphasize those who would appeal to the interviewee.[55] A businessman will be more impressed that the chamber of commerce has provided funding for your research than that the AFL-CIO also supports your efforts. You may downplay but you must not omit those sponsors that the interviewee may dislike. For example if asked why a certain group has given you money, you can state, "As you can see from the variety of funding sources, several different groups think this project is interesting. Fortunately we are not dependent on any one group, and in fact we have indicated to each agency that a condition for our taking its money is that it cannot interfere." This is especially effective when true.[56]

You should also consider how you will present yourself to the interviewee. *Avoid the interested-citizen approach.* Few respondents will believe that a citizen off the streets would go through all this effort just because of general interest. No doubt your motives would be called into question. Suspecting the worst, that you are somehow secretly checking up on him, the respondent will be extremely reluctant to part with any information.[57] The interested-citizen approach, additionally, lacks any real direction or focus. The respondent needs to know that there is a purpose to the study so that he does not believe he is wasting his time.[58]

You should also *avoid the reporter of facts role.* Few respondents are so naïve as to believe that people collect facts without a purpose. Without a plausible explanation for your project, the interviewee will again likely become suspicious.[59] Respondents, particularly those in public service, may also feel that they have fulfilled their duties to the public by providing press releases to the media. As a reporter of the facts, so the thought goes, you would have already been taken care of.[60]

A reasonable method for gaining the good graces of the interviewee is to *use the teach-me approach.* Presenting yourself as interested in learning, which you should be, provides the respondent with the opportunity to articulate his ideas without fear of being challenged by you. If the interviewee believes he can teach you something, he is likely to reveal more about the intricacies of his activities. The respondent will often be proud to demonstrate his knowledge to a receptive audience.[61]

At times you will encounter a resistant respondent. If the interviewee claims not to have time, there are several tactics to adopt. First you should appeal to the interests of the respondent. You may wish to emphasize the special role the respondent would play in your project. This can be done by pointing to his expertise or unique perspectives. Secondly you should sympathize with the respondent and indicate that you are willing to work around his busy schedule. Coupled with this expression of understanding, you may want to add that you are interested in him precisely because he is busy and so involved in daily operations.[62]

The respondent may also claim not to know anything about your project.

In such cases it is a good idea to *point to ways in which the interviewee can help*. For example you might suggest that particular expertise is not required; rather you are interested in the perspective of the respondent. Or you can suggest that the interviewee underestimates his own role in the organization or knowledge of a situation. In response to a clerk saying that he is only a minor figure in the organization, you might suggest that "it is the clerk the often serves as the backbone of any organization."[63]

Each time you meet the respondent, reintroduce yourself. It can never be safely assumed that the interviewee recalls who you are or what your project is. You do not have to go into your whole opening again. All you want to do is refresh his memory so that he understands why you are speaking to him.[64]

Now you will never get in the door a second time if there is not a first time. It is our sad duty to inform you that not everyone is willing to be interviewed. Not even if you follow our foolproof suggestions. Perseverance pays, but not always. What then?

Work around the obstreperous individual. See people at the same level elsewhere in the organization or in a related organization. Ask people who used to do what he does. Search for documentary evidence. Learn so much he cannot afford to do without this wonderful interview. When all else fails, you can cry a little. Anyway a project so dependent on a single person probably is not worth doing. Right?[65]

To Tape or Not to Tape

You will need to decide at some point how to record the interview. There is no right or wrong answer, only advantages and disadvantages, depending on your situation. The primary advantage of the tape recorder is that you will have everything that is said verbatim. This takes the guesswork out of writing the transcript of the interview. Tape-recording is especially important if data are extremely complex.[66] There are several downsides to taping, though. First, transcription is costly. It is estimated that transcribing takes over nine hours for every one hour of the interview. Most projects would not be able to afford this; nor would the costs necessarily be justified.[67] Notes taken at the time that indicate key words and turns of phrases and then filled in immediately after the interview will usually be sufficient for your purposes.[68] There is a second drawback to taping the interviewing. Often the respondent will behave differently with the tape recorder on than if he were speaking to you. Williams quite accurately describes what can happen when you use the tape recorder: "My informant was familiar with them [tape recorders] and had no objection, and as I switched it on I could see him square his shoulders—

literally—to Speak to History.''[69] Ted Lascher says that low batteries, a poor machine (not unknown among students), and background noise can defeat an interview. Whether you should join him in a fail-safe technique— note taking while interviewing—we cannot say.

If you decide to use a tape recorder, Gorden suggests explaining to the interviewee why you are using a recorder rather than asking if you can use it. Asking if it is okay to tape the conversation may raise doubts in the respondent's mind (''you mean there may be something wrong with taping the interview?''). Better to indicate that taping is a routine procedure by stating something to this effect: ''I am interested in getting all the details of your story in precisely your own words. Since I can't take shorthand the best way is to let the tape recorder do all the work.''[70] This is marginally all right. We prefer to *ask: It is the polite (and the right) thing to do.*[71]

The Written Interview

Those who (like the authors of this chapter) prefer to take notes during the interview may find certain hints helpful. Note taking is an art that can be developed only by practice. Discipline (and not a little muscle in the fingers) is essential. *Train for note taking as you would an athletic contest: jogging or aerobics are especially recommended.* The reason is that note taking, especially when doing several interviews a day, taxes the body as well as the mind. Interviewing is a physical and a mental activity. One reason we do not recommend taping is that it leads the interviewer to bad habits.[72]

One lives with the interview by immediately writing out a full account. Coffee shops are ideal for this purpose, but parked cars, bathrooms, window ledges, or anything handy can be used. Remember: With every moment that passes, a nuance of the interview may be lost.[73] Good form in interviewing also requires the interview to have been written up that very night, for that is the only way to preserve as much detail as humanly possible. The pain involved is worthwhile because the threefold repetition of each interview—taking it down for content and key phrases, writing more of it in longhand, and typing it—burns the content into memory. It creates the familiarity essential for making creative use of the contents.[74]

You should also comment on any ideas that arose during the interview. Did the respondent refer to an issue that needs to be covered in future interviews? Or was something said that might be covered in a different project? The write-up should also include, as already noted, evaluations of the interviewee's comments (hunches about perceptions that may have colored his responses) and a summary of his general disposition (angry, pleasant, satisfied).[75]

Once typed (whether previously taped or not), *the interview should be photocopied,* since interviews are valuable research material that, for safety's sake, should be kept in more than one place. They should also be locked up to preserve confidentiality. This precaution is the more necessary because *interviews should be read and reread in order to sink in, thus decreasing the chance of loss or mutilation.*[76]

Since people act on the world as they perceive it, the researcher who wishes to understand behavior must try to get under the skin. There is no better way of encouraging identification with the respondent, to think as he thinks and feel as he feels, than living the interview in the manner we have described.

Rapport and Neutrality

It is important to develop rapport with the respondent. The interviewer must be able to "imaginatively place himself in another's role and situation in order to understand the other's feelings, point of view, attitudes, and tendencies to act in a given situation.[77] Rapport cultivates mutual regard. If you recognize the peculiar problems and concerns of the respondent, he is apt to feel like he is being treated with respect rather than as an instrument for your ends. Your concern may well be reciprocated: The interviewee may try harder to remember and may disclose more intimate, previously unanticipated information. Contrarily to act unconcerned about the interviewee's feelings is to court disaster: At best the interview will be strained and the respondent indifferent to your interests; at the worst the interviewee can become unfriendly and antagonistic. Rapport is not something that you can instantly achieve; there are no simple steps to memorize; instead the literature indicates some measures you can take or avoid that may improve the possibility of establishing empathetic contact with the respondent.

When you enter an interview, the respondent will have certain expectations about your role. A blue-collar worker may pejoratively refer to you as a "know-nothing intellectual." A conservative may view all college professors as liberal. Interviewers may well be antipathetic to the attitudes of a bigot. While there is the call to remain neutral in interviewing,[78] to declare yourself neutral to, say, the Ku Klux Klansman would be the kiss of death. You will immediately be brandished as a foe, and the interview will end before it ever gets under way. The problem the interviewer frequently faces is, in the words of Dexter, "On whose side shall I be neutral?" The answer is, according to Dexter, "Where possible [. . .] accept the informant's definition of neutrality, for there is great respect, in American culture at least, for neutrality, and to be neutral in the informant's terms.[79] Much as we respect Dexter, from whom we have learned a great deal, *we prefer to be neutral, period.* For the interviewer is also a social actor. Encouraging evil may not be the idea, but it can still be the consequence.[80]

Neutrality requires you to *withhold judgment on the views of the respondent.* This means you need to restrain your anger toward the bigot and keep your views on trade policy quiet. You do not want to leave the impression that you are against the respondent, and you certainly do not want to turn the interview into a debate.[81] You are not teaching but trying to learn from the respondent. It requires discipline to keep from reacting to opinions hostile to your own. More difficult than keeping your opinions to yourself, though, is guarding against subconscious prejudice on your part.

> We may hear only what we expect to hear, basing our expectations on all sorts of cues—the speaker's voice or diction or mannerisms or dress, or something he said at another time, or what other people he seems to resemble have said. We may listen only for what fits into our purposes, leaving off as soon as we have classified the speaker . . . or satisfied our wandering curiosity, or decided what we ourselves are going to say.[82]

The best advice we have for both keeping your opinions to yourself and for mitigating prejudice is not a negative injunction (grit your teeth and bear it), but to *think about the interview as a genuine opportunity for intellectual discovery.*[83] To aid you in this endeavor, you might also speculate beforehand about such a wide range of possible responses that almost nothing could surprise you (although you will no doubt be surprised).[84]

Neutrality does not preclude understanding. You should attempt to *place yourself in the same frame of mind as the informant.* By carefully observing the actions, language, and intonation of the interviewee, you should be able to detect his demeanor. For example an executive may convey a businesslike air or an auto worker may act indignant toward people who buy foreign cars. You will want to become "a kind of verbal mirror reflecting the subject's expression back to him.[85] Simply nodding your head and being a good listener is not enough. You need to be responsive to the informant by indicating that you follow his concerns and understand why he feels that way. "Comments or questions that indicate that he [the interviewer] understands the significant features of the situation *as they appear to the respondent,* usually encourage the respondent to amplify and reveal the deeper nooks and crannies that he might at first hesitate to tell a relative stranger.[86] Kahn does a nice job of explaining that understanding does not require being like the respondent.

The interviewer must be persuaded as "within range"—that is, he must be seen as a person to whom the respondent's statement and experience will not be foreign or offensive. This does not mean that the respondent needs to see the interviewer as similar to himself, but he must view the interviewer as capable of understanding his point of view, and of doing so without rejecting him.[87]

In fact Becker even goes so far as to suggest that "the interviewer should appear to agree, or at least to empathize, with most of what the respondent tells him—no matter how outrageous or offensive it is to the interviewer."[88] Though we are loathe to disagree with such a great ethnographer as Becker, we think empathy-as-passive-approval is out but empathy-as-understanding is in.[89]

Be careful though. Lurking behind assuming a role is the danger that the respondent will begin playing to your reactions. To avoid this situation, *keep in mind that the role you assume is intended to display neutrality, not partisanship.* Play roles with moderation. In other words when confronting the businesslike executive, he may well be more responsive if you similarly conduct yourself efficiently and somewhat formally. Contrarily a jovial individual may feel uncomfortable with such formal pretensions.[90]

Part of establishing rapport with the interviewee is to *use the vernacular of the respondent.* By employing the local jargon, the respondent may feel free to speak spontaneously without having to translate for you. If the interviewee believes that you do not have a good understanding of the environment, he is likely to spend more time rephrasing his statements and going over basic terminology. More than likely the respondent will feel that it is a waste of time to go into great detail with someone who does not appear to have a good grasp of the issues.[91] Using the respondent's language can also promote good feelings. An interviewee will feel more comfortable with someone who speaks his language, since the interviewer will appear more familiar.[92]

Unless you can use the jargon to good effect, however, it is better to forego the playacting and be yourself. By using the vocabulary incorrectly, you risk confusing the respondent and further widening the gap between what the interviewee means and what you believe he means.[93] The risk of being thought a phony has to be weighed against the lesser likelihood of being thought a local type. Kahn notes this when he writes, "Teaching new language to the respondent is difficult and risky, and attempts to assume the respondent's vocabulary are more often ridiculous than effective." It is more important to be genuinely understanding than filled with colloquialisms.[94]

The foundations for the development of rapport start early in the interviewing process. *You should become aware of the respondent's situation and experiences before the interview.* Knowledge can be obtained from reading (for example newspapers may mention tense times in an administration), from speaking with other researchers and colleagues of the interviewee, and by communicating directly with him. The more knowledge you have, the greater the likelihood that you will become aware of potential obstacles to conducting a successful interview.[95]

Obstacles can crop up anywhere in the interviewing process. You should *be aware of potentially touchy subjects.* Explosive topics abound; for example the respondent may be guarded about his past job performance and become suspicious of questions about what he could have done differently. The respondent may feel guilty about his conduct; or you might uncover a particularly bitter or upsetting experience in his past.[96]

What should you do about these touchy areas? *It is best to avoid the subject if it is only marginally relevant or important to your concerns.* There is no sense upsetting the respondent and potentially ruining the interview to obtain only limited gains.[97]

If the area is important to your research, postpone those questions until the end of the interview. You want the interviewee to feel relaxed during the interview. To begin the interview with emotionally challenging questions could cause the respondent to see the encounter as hard work and consequently lose his desire to cooperate.[98] By the end of the interview, hopefully, the respondent will feel comfortable and be more willing to discuss these difficult areas.

If the interviewee appears reluctant to discuss a particular subject, do not approach the area too quickly. It is best to "talk with the respondent around the edges of the area" until the respondent leaves an opening. During the course of the interview, opportunities may arise to advance a mild question that will not upset him. Once the respondent has mentioned the high turnout in the last election, you may inquire, "How were you able to turn out such a large vote?" Compare for example that approach to asking, out of the blue, "Were there illegal actions undertaken to increase voting for your candidate."[99]

For touchy questions (as well as throughout the interview), *you should show appreciation for the respondent's efforts.* As an interviewer you are asking the respondent to spend his time, to search his memory, to work through chronologies, to answer difficult questions, and to relive memories that may be unpleasant. You can show appreciation in a number of ways. You may preface difficult questions with, "I realize how hard this question is, but I am sure you can give me some good ideas." Throughout the interview there will be occasions to praise the respondent for his effort and to comment on the good job he is doing. For example, "I know how hard it was for you to talk about these painful experiences and I appreciate it"; "you have given me an unusual amount of detail on your experiences. This is very valuable information."[100]

At the beginning of the interview as well as during it, you should *preface some questions, particularly more difficult ones, with a reminder of the respondent's qualifications.* Beginning a question with, "You have such unique insight into this problem because of your position" will support the respondent's need for recognition and provide him with confidence to answer more difficult questions.[101]

It may seem easy to overdo flattery, but experience teaches that is not so. The reasons for not being a flatterer are two: It is unbecoming and unproductive. Though the respondent will undoubtedly enjoy being flattered, his desire to retain your high opinion will lead to only his telling you more lies. *Do not flatter,* we say; it will get you somewhere, all right, but not where you want to go.[102]

Despite the many virtues of establishing rapport with the respondent, *you should not develop overrapport.* At all times you want to remain detached enough so that you can observe the respondent's behavior and statements. You do not want to become so friendly and chatty with the interviewee that you begin spontaneously responding to him without being conscious of your reactions or of the cause of those reactions.[103]

Encouragements, while useful for showing interest in what the respondent is saying, can also produce irrelevant or distorted responses. An interviewee who has little to say may feel compelled to speak because of your support.[104] Related to this, the respondent may perceive your rapport as support for a particular response and consequently be reluctant to answer contrary to these perceptions. *To avoid influencing responses, do not regularly use such encouragements as "excellent idea" or "good"; instead respond with less obvious interjections like "yes."*[105]

Do not feed the respondent your own line; there is no sense in listening to echoes of your own voice, but lots of interviewers do it. A good reason for writing down questions in advance is to spot inadvertent bias. Another good reason for rereading interviews is to make sure you are not leading the interview to a predetermined conclusion.[106]

Interviewing as Conversation or Guided Monologue?

In many ways an interview is like a conversation (although we will see later why this metaphor can be dangerous).[107] Importantly *the interview should not become an interrogation.* Interviewees tend not to like a barrage of questions that make them feel they are being cross-examined. One step toward avoiding the trial atmosphere is to let the interviewee set his own pace rather than to have you pump him for information.[108] You should also be attentive to the respondent and responsive to what is being said. Dexter suggests handling the interview "as discussion—two reflective men trying to find out how things happen, but the less informed and experienced one (the interviewer) deferring to the wiser one and learning from him."[109] In this way you may be able to create an atmosphere of spontaneity on both sides.[110]

The interview also resembles a conversation, since it reflects a "balance of revelation and concealment of thoughts and intentions." In an interview just as in a conversation, neither side completely reveals his intentions or uses words that can be taken entirely at face value. The interviewer will use general phrases to see how the respondent interprets these questions. The interviewee will play with the interviewer, testing the response to particular answers (were you shocked, sympathetic?), hiding his thoughts, and gradually revealing more as he becomes comfortable.[111]

Despite the similarities between interviewing and conversation, the metaphor is limited and more importantly can be misleading. Unlike a conversation where both participants are engaged in talking for the sheer joy of discussion, *in an interview you have a purpose in speaking with the respondent*. Think about your daily conversations (not scheduled meetings or appointments): They occur spontaneously; you do not go into the conversation with a prepared agenda, and the discussion freely flows to whatever interests the two of you at the moment. Not so in an interview. While you may create the illusion of spontaneous dialogue, the truth is that the interviewer and interviewee are instruments serving their own ends. You are speaking to the respondent because he has information that you need for your project. And he may want to get his views across to the public.[112]

Another reason that an interview is not quite like a conversation, particularly one between friends, is that you and the respondent are usually strangers. And this is good. *You do not want to become friends with the respondent.* This does not mean that you should not be friendly; rather the expectation of the interviewee should be that he will not see you again. It is often easier for the interviewee to reveal more intimate secrets to someone he will never face again nor hear from than to speak to a friend. The respondent does not have to worry so much about how a relative stranger will react to his statements, whereas telling such secrets to an acquaintance may damage the friendship.[113]

It may be better to *think of the interview as a guided monologue*. The interview is *guided,* not completely free nor completely controlled by you. You try to move the discussion toward areas that appear fruitful and away from peripheral topics.[114] The bases for your decisions on what questions to ask next are a combination of preplanning (knowing what topics you want covered) and reaction to the interviewee (when something interesting and relevant is said, pursue it).

The interview is also a *monologue,* not a conversation. Unlike a conversation, you do not reveal your views. *When asked for your opinion, it is best to appear to answer the question without really stating your own beliefs.* When asked, "What do you think of that?" it is preferable to say, "It *is* hard to form an opinion on that, isn't it? What do you think?" than to give your opinion or to say, "We aren't allowed to express our beliefs."[115] Expressing your views may bias the interviewee. Saying that you cannot give your opinion, while necessary when the respondent insists on knowing what you think, should be avoided, since it can sound unnecessarily argumentative. The following scenario is quite possible:

Respondent: What do you think?
Interviewer: I can't state what I think.
Respondent: Why not?
Interviewer: Because I should remain neutral.
Respondent: But you do have beliefs, so you aren't neutral.

Uh oh! You have lost control of the interview.

Unlike a conversation the preponderance of the interview should consist of the interviewee speaking. You want to obtain information, not tell your side of the story. The expectation of the respondent that he will have "a rare opportunity to express political opinions at length and in detail without contradiction" and without having to endure "unsatisfactory, boring, or confusing conversations" may be gratifying to him.[116] *The less said by the interviewer the better.* It is optimal to allow the interviewee to speak at length and spontaneously.[117]

Do not cut the respondent off even if he wanders. That is just the time you may learn something surprising.[118] *When desperate* however, that is, when the interview is about to conclude and you have nothing to lose, *use challenge questions.* Put the matter directly to the respondent—did he or did he not?—in an effort to shock him into a response. In the end you may be the one who is shocked, or upended, but then you were not getting anywhere anyway.[119]

Asking the Right Kinds of Questions: From Opening to Probing

In an open-ended interview, all questions are not created equal. Certain types of questions work better in different parts of the interview or with different people. While your opening questions are designed to set the respondent at ease, the purpose of questions that introduce new subjects is to locate potential areas of significant data. Consequently you should *introduce topics and subtopics with broad questions*. These prevent the interviewer from accidentally restricting the scope of the inquiry. For example instead of starting your questioning with, "What did you do when . . . ?" you will likely obtain more information by initially inquiring, "What happened when . . . ?" You can later follow up by asking what he did. Broad questions often stimulate the respondent's memory by encouraging him to think about the topic as a whole. It is possible through the use of open questions to create an atmosphere where the respondent is encouraged to think aloud, to fill in the blank page that the unstructured question represents.[120] Contrarily when asked a very narrow question, the respondent may limit his answer, leaving other potentially relevant information untapped. Worse, a series of specific questions may cause the respondent to make up answers to please the interviewer (and to not appear ignorant).[121]

You should also *introduce topics and subtopics with unstructured questions*. Use questions that do not suggest the expected answer in the wording of the question. In other words do not feed the respondent the answer. Rather than asking, "Was it this way or that way?" try stating the question so that the respondent must choose his own alternative (for example, "Why did these people leave the organization?" instead of, "Did these people leave because they disliked the head of the organization?"). Significant data may very well turn up where you least expect it.[122]

Introduce topics and subtopics with general lead questions. By starting with questions whose key words are general, you allow the interviewee to interpret the question "in his own terms, and out of his own experience."[123] Contrarily asking specific, finely worded questions requires the respondent to think and speak in the interviewer's terms rather than in his own. Accordingly, "Encouraging the respondent to focus inward, on his own thoughts and feelings, rather than outward, on the interviewer's demands and definitions, permits him to organize and express his thoughts clearly and coherently.[124] Consider some typical lead questions: "How did you feel about the people you worked with?" or "What impressed you about how the organization was run?" The interviewee's interpretation of the general question may be quite revealing of the interviewee's perspectives and concerns.

Use short questions, the shorter, the better. Long involved questions breed uncertain answers. Neither the respondent nor the interviewer will know exactly what the response means. This is easier said than done. Self-correction is essential. When you cannot make sense of an answer on rereading, change the question.[125] One of our favorites (to officials in spending departments) was, "How do you decide how much to ask for?"

and (to congressmen) "How do you decide what to give?" The suggestion that the money was theirs to give was deliberate; Congress does exercise the power of the purse, and congressmen like to be reminded of it. Unto this day.

The exception proves the rule. British ministers responded well to the question, "Ministers are rated by how well they do in getting money for their departments from Cabinet. I understand you do (or did) especially well. How did (or do) you do it?"

A mistake that many interviewers make is launching into a lengthy explanation of the question or stating the questions in several different ways without providing the interviewee an opportunity to respond. Do not follow this sequence: "What have been the effects of this new legislation? I mean, it is anticipated that the new law will increase paper work and your office is already overburdened." Usually a question should take no more than two sentences (and preferably one sentence).[126] And be sure to ask only one question at a time. You will get only confused answers, since the respondent must grapple with organizing his statement to several questions instead of just one.[127]

Answers to general questions are helpful for uncovering how the respondent weighs the relative importance of different factors, revealing the frame of reference (does he see himself as secretly in charge, a victim, misunderstood?) and discovering vocabulary.[128]

During the course of the interview, it is important for you to understand how the respondent is using particular terms and what assumptions he has about the question. This is one of many conflicting demands placed on the interviewer. On the one hand, broad general questions are useful for soliciting unanticipated responses and stimulating the respondent's memory; on the other hand, such questions, by their very nature, leave many terms only implicitly defined. If you as the interviewer do not ferret out these underlying assumptions, you risk talking past each other or assuming the respondent's answers say one thing when they actually mean another.

There is no easy way out of this difficulty, but you can minimize the tradeoff by *actively listening.* By this we do not mean passively receiving the words and jotting them down. Rather you must concentrate on the conversation as it is going on. Sidney and Beatrice Webb accurately describe what it means to listen attentively.

The first, indispensable factor in successful investigation or fruitful observation . . . is an efficient attention. . . . Few (for instance even in listening to lectures) seem to "take in" more than a small proportion of the statements made by the lecturer or even to absorb . . . the points he has most strenuously endeavored to drive home. To quote, "people hear some isolated point and instead of listening to the sentences that follow it, they proceed to build upon it *some notion of their own* of what the speaker is trying to say; and *this notion is what they attend to,* finding a confirmation of it in any fragments which reach their minds afterwards. In fact, they theorise, instead of trying to experience; and usually their theory is based on their own experience, not on the (presently hearable) facts so that from all speaking, *they get only what they have brought to it,* and this is not what the speaker said."[129]

By paying careful attention to the conversation, you may be able to pick up hints about the respondent's underlying assumptions or beliefs. These hints may take the form of vocabulary used (*Negroes* rather than *blacks, Mexicans,* not *Chicanos, lovers* versus *perverts*), references to groups (damn Yankees), adjectives or adverbs used (she's *only* a housewife, I'm a *proud* American), as well as direct statements of beliefs (I consider myself to be a conservative on social issues). *If unsure of particular assumptions held by the respondent or if you feel the assumptions need to be further developed, you may wish to ask questions that directly address the underlying beliefs.* You might ask, "What did you mean by 'damn Yankees'?" or, "Why do you consider yourself 'conservative on social issues'?" if the answer to these questions will shed light on the responses of the interviewee.[130] It is better to ask about specific views because the respondent may not be able to answer a developmental question that has stumped scholars for generations.[131]

Asking only broad, ambiguous questions will likely result in receiving information limited in depth. *While the interview is going on, the interviewer should probe or clarify the meaning of the answers.* Before turning to methods of probing, it is necessary to recognize that effective probing is next to impossible if you see yourself as a passive recipient of data. [132]

As an interviewer you must actively participate in the information-gathering activity. This means that you should *reflect on what is being said, be alert to what appears to be jumps in logic, and be aware of general and ambiguous comments.* By focusing your attention on the respondent, you will be better able to detect inconsistencies and ambiguities. Additionally, according to Dexter, "concentrated attention" involves the ability to

shift gears rapidly; that is to say, when the interviewee makes what seem to him [the interviewer] to be a jump, he must not show any feeling that there is an irrelevance, but must with one corner of his mind, note that he may need to discover how the interviewee makes the transition, while with the forefront of his attention, he is listening eagerly to what seems to be the new topic.[133]

When interviewing, move from obtaining general comments to digging out specific references that elicited these general responses. A common mistake of inexperienced interviewers is not sticking with a subject until the "good data are teased out."

> The green interviewer sometimes seems to assume that once he asks a question about something and an answer is given he should move on to the next subject. But the lead question in an area is just the first spade of dirt. If the interviewer is going to get at hidden treasures he sometimes has to unearth heaps of useless dirt before he strikes gold.[134]

If the interviewee says he is unhappy with how he is treated, ask for specific examples of his mistreatment. Charles Morrissey emphasizes that it is important to obtain examples, "One guideline I would stress, perhaps above all others, is that a good interviewer should pursue *in detail,* constantly asking for examples, constantly asking people to illustrate points they are making."[135] Asking the respondent to illustrate his points serves several purposes. It allows you to draw your own inferences. It provides some measure for verifying the accuracy of the interviewee's general statements. And, importantly, asking for concrete examples can often stimulate the respondent's memory by transporting him back to the time when these experiences occurred. Through "retrospective introspection" the respondent reexperiences the situation. By probing to encourage a network of associations, the interviewer can aid the respondent in recalling specific details as well as reporting his reactions and feelings at the time.[136]

Once you discover a fruitful area, stick with it. Even if it means that you may have to sacrifice breadth of coverage, you should not pass up valuable occasions when the respondent opens up and provides you with rich data. There is a better chance that you can return to subjects you did not cover on another day, but you will probably not be able to recreate the situation that led to the revelations.[137]

Once you have adequately covered the material for your purposes, dismiss that line of inquiry and move on. You certainly do not want to bore the respondent by pursuing a subject long after he has lost interest. Furthermore putting aside the line of questioning allows you to concentrate on the next subject.[138]

Of all questions probes are the easiest to ask—Why? What other reasons are there? What else? Can you give an example? Another example would be helpful—and to miss. The inexperienced interviewer will find these opportunities passing by him faster than he can make use of them. Because experience is such a wonderful teacher, instructors and interviewers should read interviews to discuss missed opportunities. We repeat: *Reread interviews for missed opportunities in order to do better next time.*[139]

There are many different ways and reasons to probe.

1. *If the response is ambiguous or vague, you should ask for clarification.* Usually it is best and easiest to ask for clarification at the time the statement is made. If the respondent states, "A lot of people work here," a clarifying question would follow, "How many people would you say work here?"[140]

If the respondent has broached a potentially fruitful topic before you have a chance to ask for clarification, *do not interrupt the flow of the interview.* Let him finish his thought and then go back to missed points or general statements. By interrupting you risk disturbing the flow of the conversation, preempting potentially interesting statements, and leaving an impression that you are not willing to allow the respondent to finish his thought.[141] When you do come back to a question, be sure to indicate that you heard and understood what was said before so that the respondent does not think you were just not paying attention.[142]

2. *You can also use clarifying questions to reference feelings implicit in the interviewee's responses.* Toward the end of the questioning on a particular subject, you might inquire, for example, "Do you still feel anger toward the Japanese?" or, "Do you often feel unappreciated?"[143]

3. *Clarifying questions can be used to pursue seeming inconsistencies.* It is usually a safe assumption that the respondent believes he is thinking consistently. Yet responses given by the interviewee will often seem to conflict. Use probe questions to uncover reasons why apparently inconsistent beliefs can be held simultaneously.[144] It is usually best not to challenge aggressively the respondent, since such confrontations will either make him feel stupid or defensive, thereby causing him to be more inhibited in expressing himself. Instead phrase the question so that it does not sound as though you are judging the answers. Rather than, "How can you possibly explain this contradiction?" it will be more effective to state, "I am a little confused on this point. Before you said that . . . Could you clarify these two statements for me?"[145]

4. *You may elicit additional information through the echo.* An echo is created by repeating the respondent's words with a rising inflection at the end of your question. For instance an interviewee might state, "I was unhappy with my job," to which you might echo, "You were unhappy?" An echo should be used only when the prior response is relevant to the interview, since an echo encourages the respondent to continue speaking about the same subject matter. An echo is appropriate only when you believe the respondent has more to say.[146] Needless to say not all respondents enjoy this application of Rogerian therapy.[147]

5. *You can also obtain additional information through extension.* An extension refers back to information a respondent has already provided.

You may desire to know the respondent's feelings about an event he just described primarily in factual terms. Thus you might follow the description of the situation by inquiring, "Tell me how you felt during all this."[148] An extension may also be used to return to an earlier topic that you did not fully pursue because of resistance by the interviewee. The respondent may later be more confident or more emotionally involved in an issue and consequently willing to discuss the particular topic.[149]

6. *You may summarize what has been said to increase the coherence of a response.* If you are not sure how everything fits together, you can formulate what you believe to be an accurate summary of what has been said and explicitly or implicitly request confirmation or correction. It is usually best to preface your summary by suggesting that you are not sure if you fully understand. This will open the door for the respondent to improve on your summary, since it will be clear that you do not have any ego invested in your statements.[150]

7. *Challenge questions can be used to increase clarity or validity.* You may encounter situations when an interviewee provides two conflicting responses or when one answer contradicts information known to be true. Examples of challenge questions include, "How do you reconcile these conflicting statements?" or "According to the financial report, you actually receive more contributions from them than from anyone else." The confrontation poses an obvious danger: The respondent may feel threatened by the cross-examination and restrain his discussion. But a challenge question may also be regarded by some participants, particularly those who are confident or enjoy argument, as an indication of your interest and attention to what the respondent has said.[151]

Asking a challenge question does not mean that you must sound argumentative. Continue to think about the wording of your questions. Which question do you think will get a better response: "None of this makes any sense. How can you possibly say this when previously you state . . . ?" or "I believe you said before that . . . does that conflict with your last statement?"[152]

8. *Stay away from repetitions.* You may determine that the response to the question the first time it was asked was evasive, superficial, or unreliable. The same question can be asked later in the interview to see how the second response corresponds with the first.[153] Repetitions are dangerous though, since the interviewee may remember the question was asked and be angry that you did not believe his first answer. Besides, the purpose of repetition can be served by rephrasing the question.[154]

Use probe notes to keep track of areas that need further probing or clarification. In these notes write down key words and phrases so that you can use the respondent's own words when following up. Using the vocabulary of the respondent will indicate to him that you are paying attention and can be useful for jarring his memory. "What did you mean when you said, 'Congress is micromanaging the defense budget'?" sounds like you are attentive and will more likely trigger his memory than, "You said something about Congress and the military. What did you mean?" Even if you are using a tape recorder, these notes are important for keeping track of points to be covered or probed as well as for providing a reference to vocabulary used.[155]

Once you ask the question, keep quiet and wait for the answer. The silence that follows, while embarrassing in everyday conversation, is often quite useful in obtaining precious information. John Dean explains the virtues of the pregnant pause:

> The interviewer should have the perspicacity to *wait out the pregnant silences.* When in doubt as to what to say or what to ask, many interviewers just *pause.* If not sure what to say he may say the wrong thing—or, more likely and even worse, he may cut off some crucial data the respondent was hesitating to reveal. "Dead air" presents a powerful invitation to jump in, and will often precipitate data a respondent had not intended to reveal.[156]

How long should a silence be held before it becomes too embarrassing and inhibits the interview? If the respondent completes a sentence with a "tone of finality and then looks at the interviewer expectantly, a two-second pause assures that he has finished the comment. . . ." On the other hand, if the respondent stops in midsentence or midthought or appears to be pausing to think, a silence of ten seconds may be more appropriate.[157]

Provide definitions to difficult terms in a question. It is better to provide definitions discretely if there is doubt that the person will understand the terms. By this we mean including the definition in the context of the question. It is better to say, "As you may be aware, there has been a move to permit prisoners to be allowed more intimate visits with their spouses. What do you think of these conjugal visits?" than to ask, "What are your views on conjugal visits? If you do not know, a conjugal visit is. . . ." Placing the definition within the context of your question will not put the respondent in the uncomfortable position of having to ask what the question means or of making it appear that you think the respondent does not know the definition. By providing definitions you also avoid the danger that the interviewee will pretend to know the meaning of a term (when in fact he does not), resulting in irrelevant and uninformative answers.[158]

The interviewer must carefully balance providing too many definitions, thus defeating the goal of ambiguous questions, with providing too few definitions. A good way to avoid this dilemma is to *shun difficult terms when introducing topics and later use these terms as you move to more specific questions and gain an idea of the respondent's vocabulary.*[159]

While you will normally ask questions that do not suggest a possible answer, there are times when leading questions can be useful. These intimate a particular answer. During the course of the interview (particularly toward its end), you may discover occasions when you think the respondent is withholding information because it goes against widely held beliefs. In this case *leading questions are helpful if they result in answers that are contrary to public ideals.*[160] What is contrary to public ideals may include anything from views on race relations to attitudes toward loyalty to political administrations. For example you may believe that the respondent is holding back his opinion that he wished the Second World War would have continued because he was economically benefiting from it. A leading question to elicit discussion of this attitude might be, "You were doing so well during the war. Do you not sometimes wish it would have continued?"

In effect leading questions encourage the respondent to express ideas or reveal information that he would otherwise be reluctant to state. Be careful. *Do not use leading questions that result in answers consonant with public ideals.* The danger is that the respondent will simply agree with the slanted questions (even though he does not really agree), since it is easier to conform than to appear deviant.[161]

In general *be alert to subtle clues that indicate the respondent is withholding or distorting his answers to please you.* This is certainly not an easy task but a talent that can improve through experience. For example watch for conflicting statements, for occasions when the interviewee begins to respond, then holds back the statement, or for seemingly minor phrases that suggest a particular outlook. A good instance of the latter example is when an auto worker who acted strongly anti-Japanese around other workers stops using the term Japs in private.[162]

Drawing Conclusions

A good interview requires you not only to ask penetrating questions, but also to draw conclusions from these responses. *Do not expect the respondent to spell out your conclusions for you.* Like a detective you must piece together the bits of information provided by different respondents. The answer you reach may be different from the conclusions of all the people you have interviewed.[163]

Part of drawing conclusions is determining how the respondent sees the situation. There are two aspects to the interviewee's perceptions that should be kept in mind. First, prior experiences and predispositions affect how the respondent perceives his environment. *You cannot be expected to deduce the entire life of the respondent, but you should be aware of clues about past experiences that color responses.*[164] Some potential areas to examine are his ethnicity and national background.[165] Does the interviewee see himself as overworked, the only competent person in his organization, maligned by others? Does the individual enjoy his work and the people he interacts with, or does he feel his time is wasted and his peers are unappreciative? Are there previous salient experiences that would affect the respondent's outlook, such as having been fired from the organization he is discussing? Is the occupation of the respondent affecting how the past is viewed? For example there is a "strong propensity of politicians to interpret the past in the light of the present," which "makes it impossible to accept all they say at face value."[166] Researching the organization and person you will interview ahead of time will aid you in this task. It is also necessary to be alert to the respondent's statements and word choices: "No one appreciates me around here" is a dead giveaway. More subtly the interviewee might mention, "Others have left because no one recognized their importance." If important for your project, you should then follow up with, "Do you feel that no one recognizes your importance to this organization?"

Another aspect of the interviewee's perceptions is his conception of his audience. Thus a member of Congress may react differently to an interviewer he believes is interested in (and would appreciate the intricacies of) political strategy as opposed to someone concerned with public service (who would be less impressed by tales of maneuvering and dissimulation). Interviewees are usually quite good at picking up your particular slant or predisposition, so be careful about your facial expressions, how you word questions, your verbal responses, and miscellaneous comments you make. As before, act as a reflection of the respondent.[167]

Drawing conclusions also requires you to pay attention to how questions are answered. Insightful listening, as Doby describes it, "enables one to analyze and interpret what is being said—to piece together the little clues that reveal what is *meant* or *implied* by the respondent."[168] The inexperienced interviewer will often be content to simply get down whatever is said, often missing what might be behind these statements.

What should you look for? *Watch for areas where the respondent shows emotional involvement.* Affect is often revealed by a trembling voice, changes in bodily and facial tension (increased tension when angry, a look of resignation when sad or disappointed), stammering, watery eyes, long silences, protestation or heavy emphasis on certain points, or defensiveness.[169] Understanding responses of central significance to the interviewee will be helpful in evaluating his beliefs.[170] You will also want to discriminate between opinions weakly held (and verbalized only because asked) from those strongly held, because the former opinions will yield little detail (and may likely result in the respondent making up things as he goes along), whereas the latter are likely to produce a mine of information.[171]

Also watch for glib responses. A respondent will sometimes provide articulate explanations that serve as justifications or rationalizations for actions. Some phrases to watch for include, "Since everyone was doing it"; "I did as I was instructed to. I think following orders is extremely important to the efficient operation of an organization"; or, "I felt I was acting in the best interests of everyone concerned." Rarely will it be to your benefit to challenge such a response. It is far better to let the respondent complete his explanation; once he feels more secure, he may be willing to discuss his doubts and concerns.[172]

After the interview you will want to *recapture these reactions.* When writing up and analyzing the interview, provide general comments about the reactions of the respondent. For instance you might point out, "The respondent disliked academics intensely, so perhaps the statement should be evaluated accordingly," or, "He seems still to resent his ex-boss, most likely because his boss fired him."[173]

The interviewer must constantly be alert to considerations that are likely to slant a respondent's perceptions and answers. You must not only record what is told and compare it to what others have said, you must also weigh the intrinsic value of the statement.[174] Does the explanation sound plausible, or are important points left out or attenuated? Any parent has learned to weigh the intrinsic merits of statements by teens arriving home late at night. So, too, we received a lesson on the plausibility of certain responses during the Iran–Contra hearings.

There is a danger in evaluating the authenticity of an interviewee's comments. Once the interviewer engages in weighing the merits of explanations, the interviewer "has always to be on his guard against an insidious temptation in his own mind: that he may unconsciously fiddle the weights, attaching too much importance to testimony which suits his own presuppositions or prejudices, and too little to that which he finds inconvenient."[175] Easier said than done. A guard (but by no means a guarantee) against projecting your expectations into a response is to *be conscious of your own predispositions.*[176] You may believe that every comment politicians make is designed to further their chances for reelection. But do not let this belief color you evaluation of comments made in a particularly revealing or reflective moment.

The Great Deceiver

What do you do when during the course of the interview, you realize that the respondent is deceiving you? The problem arises less from deliberate lying (though that has occurred) than from honest opinions mistakenly held.[177] There are some obvious indicators of deception: conflicting statements, statements that you know to be untrue, evasiveness, and a story that does not quite add up. You should also watch for less clear-cut indicators of doubtful statements, such as a tendency to exaggerate or an inability to provide concrete examples for generalizations made. If a partisan suggests, "The previous administration destroyed the civil service" yet is unable to produce one instance of how the service has changed, then doubt may be cast on the basis for the interviewee's belief. The respondent may have made the statement to make the other administration look bad or because he had heard this from someone else. He may even be right, but to use a baseless opinion is unwise.[178]

There are several ways to guard against deception. Preparing before the interview is an important first step. Researching the organization and the individual as well as speaking to others will help you evaluate responses.[179] Letting the respondent speak freely will often help you identify inauthentic comments. If the respondent must explain his ideas in detail, there is a greater likelihood that you will uncover inconsistencies or unsupported generalities that are then ground for further investigation.[180]

When the respondent uses percentages, it is a good idea to translate them into numbers. There is a tendency to overestimate when using percentages. Thus if the respondent states that 90 percent of the people in the organization belong to a club, and you know there are a hundred people in the organization, ask if he means 90 people are members. It may well be that he really only knows of 50 or 60. You should also be alert to the human tendency to exaggerate long distances or periods of time.[181] You may also prevent falsification by suggesting to the respondent that you know the score. Letting him know that you understand what was done or that you are aware of certain information may save the interviewee from having to erect a complex facade to hide his actions and then maintain the story for fear of being considered a liar.[182] There are subtle ways of indicating your knowledge of delicate situations. Rather than stating, "I know all about corruption in your organization," which would have the effect of immediately placing the interviewee on the defensive, it would be better to indicate, "I know how difficult it is to run an organization without rewarding those who are loyal to you."

Establishing shared goals will also go a long way toward ensuring the validity of responses. If you can get the respondent to recognize that you are both interested in arriving at a complete picture of events, then the interviewee may "exert himself to the utmost to provide accurate information."[183]

In addition to asking the interviewee questions about content, you should *ask the respondent who else you should also speak to.* The suggestions given can be helpful in uncovering potential interviewees that you had not thought to see. The respondent's suggestions can also reveal interrelationships: Those named are often his friends or frequent contacts. Do not worry if the interviewee says that he does not think a particular individual will speak to you. A supposedly reluctant person will often see you.[184] *Use the cobweb method; go from one person who recommends you to another until you have unearthed the relevant network and achieved your goal.*

Calling It Quits

When to call a halt to an interview pales in importance before when to stop interviewing. Ideally you should follow the *rule of diminishing returns: Stop interviewing about a unit, position, or person when there are no more surprises.* When you keep hearing what you have heard before, it is time to move on. In real life there are reasons extrinsic to research that limit interviewing: time, money, patience, energy. There is no prescription to offer here, since life tells you to stop because you have run out of a vital resource.

Determining how long to interview someone is influenced by several variables. You will need to judge how busy the respondent is. Does he have pressing business to attend to? Have new appointments arrived? Has the respondent made references like, "I feel really backlogged with my work" or, "As you can see by the piles of papers, I barely get any sleep as it is"? You must also evaluate the attitude of the respondent toward the interview. Is he enjoying it or does he seem impatient? You should remember though that even if the interviewee says that you can stay (and even if he appears eager), the respondent may later come to resent how much time he spent with you. Furthermore the interviewee may just be acting politely toward you, like the relationship between hosts and guests who have overstayed their welcome. Generally speaking it is risky to stretch the interview beyond 45 minutes. If you have not completed your questions and there is a chance to come back later, you can inquire if it is okay to speak to him in a few days for some more details.[185]

Be alert. At the end of an interview, the respondent may feel more at ease because the questioning is over. Often revealing comments will be made or information will come out that the respondent did not feel was important at the time.[186]

When you close your notebook or shut off your tape recorder, however, your body language suggests the formal interview is over and the rest is off-the-record. Do not fall into deviousness. Stop your interview; like the great Yogi, act like "it's over when it's over."

End the interview with a brief conversation. This gives the interviewee an opportunity to provide rationalizations for statements he now has second thoughts about making. This may preempt retaliation later on when the respondent tells others to watch out for you because you force things out of your interviewees.[187] During the conversation you should also assuage any fears of the respondent (about confidentiality, about what you think of him because of some of his comments, and so on) and make some final statement about your appreciation for the interviewee's time and helpfulness.[188]

Provide assurances of confidentiality. You should do this at the beginning and end of the interview as well as at selected times during the interview when the respondent appears to be hesitating to speak because he fears the information will become public.[189]

Gorden says that it is not necessary to offer all respondents confidentiality; however confidentiality is a good idea if the respondent will not speak unless he remains anonymous; if you believe the interviewee's statements will be slanted by the knowledge that his name will be made public (for example, he may try to make himself look good for the public record or tone down his views because of feared repercussions); or if speaking will jeopardize his well being.[190] We think that the interviewer can go either way but that *whether or not the interview is confidential should be made absolutely clear to the respondent.*

Afterward if a quotation from the respondent is desired in your written text, there are two ways to handle this. *You may find something similar in a public document, a newspaper, court proceedings, or legislative hearing that is bolstered by your private interview,* or *you may ask the respondent for permission to quote,* giving not only the actual words but also the surrounding context. Truth in advertising applies to researchers as well as to other people trying to make their way in the world.

After your meeting *keep track of who sees the interview.* Assurances of confidentiality should be respected. Ethically it is your responsibility to fulfill your promise. Practically it is not only embarrassing but potentially damaging to your credibility for future interviews. Interviews will quickly dry up if word gets out that you cannot be trusted.[191]

Preparing Interviews for Writing

By this time you have collected 80 to 90 percent of the material. You cannot be sure whether you have collected too much or too little. Following the guidelines you have numbered each interview. On three-by-five cards, you have written the number, full name, title, address, phone number, and biographical data about each interview and locked away these cards to maintain confidentiality. You also have a file of written sources. On four-by-six cards, you have written ideas for organization or analysis as they came to you for the article or book you are contemplating writing. What next?

Empty your mind of ideas for organizing this work by writing chapter or section headings (approximations will do). Keep it simple; you will likely change your mind. A heading alone or a few sentences at most describing content will suffice. Place these headings in order, shuffling cards as you go. Number the headings in pencil as if you expect to order them. Relax. Cards are easy to discard.

Read over each photocopied interview. Then go back and circle each separate thought or bit of data, marking it with what then appears to be its proper location within the manuscript. A single word or phrase as well as a paragraph or two can go on a card. The object here is to be exhaustive in mining the data, not to keep your cards neat nor to make their content equal. Then paste each bit on a separate card.

At this point some cards will not appear readily classifiable. What to do? Perhaps this process of coding (this is what it is) will suggest a need for new headings or subheadings. If so, write another number and classify accordingly; if not, put such cards aside until you can classify them or decide to discard them. Following this procedure will eventually produce not only a detailed outline but also an outline for writing.

Having treated all interviews in this manner, you can also write on separate cards new thoughts as they manifest themselves: Classify these or develop new classifications for them or just hold them in abeyance for a more insightful moment. And go through the as-yet unusable for clues of what you might have left out.

The time has come to merge the cards made from the written interviews with those from the oral interviews. Combining the two sources is bound to alter the existing but fortunately alterable scheme of classification. No, this is not a hopeless jumble but an opportunity for creative ferment. New relationships are revealed. Material previously unclassified or unclassifiable finds its place, while other material, perviously well ensconced, now needs a new home. Once again go from beginning to end, filing and refiling. Once again look through the residual and attempt to place it or find a new place for it. The remainder is not rubbish but rather an as-yet-untapped source of new concepts. Leave it until its time comes.

The first two shuffles have been devoted to rough classification. Familiarity with the material has grown. The moment for fine classification has come. Each chapter should be given headings, each section subheadings, each card placed in order of exposition. Some cards, it turns out, have multiple uses: Either photocopy them and place them where they should go or note on the first use its succeeding placements. Again these data cards will be moved around, some even moved out. Put these with the residual material and try once more to classify them. Enough unused cards should have accumulated to see if a body or data or a line of thought deserves separate consideration.

Until this third stage has been completed, you would be hard put to say what, if anything, has been left out. For what is to be included depends on the problem you wish to solve, the argument you wish to present. You cannot be entirely certain until you write, for only the act of writing itself (not every thought will be written and not everything written is a worthy thought) can fully reveal the structure of what is contemplated.

Here you face a choice: You can either conduct extra interviews and documentary research, or you can write up your account, hoping thereby to gain a truer perspective on what is needed. One way to choose is by the availability of sources; if they are unlikely to be available later, use them now. Another consideration is the availability of your personal resources. It may be best to postpone interviews and travel until time and money and energy are available. Whatever the choice the new material should be incorporated into the old.

After you have finished each draft, review the unused cards; throw them out when they obviously do not fit. When there are no more cards left, you are near completion. Keep your cards until the article or book is published; they are invaluable when checking footnotes. But do not discard ideas. The card that was rejected, as the Bible says, may become the cornerstone of a new edifice.

You may find the procedure advocated here to be exhausting. In a way that is the idea. The object is to get out of yourself every last bit of what you have to give. Later when you reread your work as a stranger, wondering who could have written it, or how you came on this idea, you have initiated yourself into the scholar's craft.

Defects of Open-Ended Interviews

Among the well-known defects of this art form is its unsystematic character. Many important factors vary in ways difficult to control: the character of the interviewer, most of all; but also the time available, the era in which the project takes place (the openness of sites differs according to the time period), the effort devoted, even luck. The ability to gain entry may depend on happenstance—the occurrence of certain events or the availability of a key person. You can rarely be certain (absent other projects covering the same ground) that other investigators would come up with the same description, let alone analysis. That is why the open-ended, semistructured interview should be thought of as a source of two types of information otherwise unavailable.

The first is the discovery of social facts, as sociologists called it long ago, namely, the location of phenomena together with an approximate description. (Immediately it should be noted that these discoveries are often contested by others who cast doubt on their size, scope, shape, and causes. A good contemporary example would be homelessness.) The second is the formulation of hypotheses about both the dependent and independent variables, what is to be explained and how it is to be explained. This understood—interviews are good for setting up, not solving, a research problem—the very subjectivity of open-ended, semistructured interviews may be considered an advantage. Their total immersion in the subject matter, we think, is an aid to creativity.

There are also lesser known but important defects of research based on this sort of interview. One of these is the subjection of interviewers to widely shared biases within the milieux they are investigating. When these biases are really significant, they are likely to be less conscious and therefore difficult to discern.

A related defect is the cooptation of researchers by the people and organizations they are studying. Other-induced cooptation takes place when a deliberate effort is made to convert a social scientist into an advocate. "Going native," however modern these natives appear, is an old story. Self-induced cooptation is a newer defect under which researchers persuade themselves they have a moral duty to act as advocates for the group they are studying. We emphatically disagree. "Doing it to yourself" is worse than being "hard done by" because you cooperate in your own corruption. Patronizing the subject population, making them into people who need you instead of you depending on them, demeans them. Patronizing your academic discipline by suggesting that its normal modes of inquiry debase worthy people demeans you. If normal science is immoral, why are you in it? Being false to your vocation in order to be true to your values is inherently corrupting. There has rightly been a reaction against those who work for intelligence agencies while pretending to be scholars. How much better is it to work against governments you do not like while pretending to be a scholar?

Using yourself as an instrument of investigation, as required by the open-ended, semistructured interview, is both a snare and an opportunity. It is a snare for those who mistakenly believe they already know what they have come to discover. It can be an opportunity for those who seek to formulate and reformulate ideas through disciplined communion with their subject matter.

Lewis Dexter and Selma Monsky remind us that interviewees also may benefit from the process. Dexter says that

> I think it is not quite true . . . that busy men are hesitant to be interviewed. Many of them find an experienced, informed interviewer very useful or rewarding . . . because many men of affairs have nobody they can talk to honestly about their task and responsibilities. Yes, they have staff, but you say something to staff and they'll quote it against you, later on. Yes, you have colleagues but there may be some rivalry. Yes, you have professional peers but you have to maintain a facade with them. So, I think a fair number of business men we interviewed—especially important business men who couldn't relax in small business organizations or at Rotary—found interviews with us worthwhile, once they got started.[192]

Selma Monsky advises that

> . . . people have a need to think through their ideas with an interested, sympathetic, non-judgmental interviewer. . . . I'm convinced that this is the primary appeal that keeps many respondents involved and participating in interviews. I still remember one of my first respondents (almost 40 years ago) thanked me because she had learned so much; when I protested that I hadn't told her anything, that she was telling me things, she agreed, adding 'But I haven't thought through some of these things before, and I've learned a lot.'[193]

The greater the mutuality, the better the experience.

As Lew Dexter emphasizes in his seminal book, interviewing is a transactional process in which a new thing is created. Each side plays to the other. There is (but there is also more than) impression management. The distance between actor and audience is constantly being reduced and enlarged. Sometimes the positions are reversed. New perceptions emerge from each other and the events and ideas under discussion. The new reality, albeit fleeting, is real. Whether it is true (or truer) matters; whether it is powerful in leading to better questions and answers matters more.

Notes

1. This is particularly true if there are several people conducting interviews. In that case, the project coordinator needs to keep in close contact with the other participants so that the objectives remain consistently defined. See Raymond L. Gorden, *Interviewing: Strategy, Technique, and Tactics* (Homewood, Ill.: Dorsey Press, 1969, 1975), p. 471.
2. Ibid., p. 472; Philip M. Williams, "Interviewing Politicians: The Life of Hugh Gaitskell," the *Political Quarterly* 51, no. 3 (July–September 1980): 303–16,

305; Walter Van Dyke Bingham and Bruce Victor Moore, *How to Interview,* 4th ed. (New York: Harper & Brothers, 1959), pp. 64–65.

3. Gorden, p. 472.
4. Robert K. Merton and Patricia L. Kendall, "The Focused Interview," *American Journal of Sociology* 51, no. 6 (May 1946): 541–57, 541.
5. Williams, "Interviewing Politicians," p. 303.
6. A. W. Seeking respondent's theories, Lewis Dexter states, can help the interviewer understand why the respondent acts as she does. (Letter to Aaron Wildavsky, undated, received December 1987.)
7. D. H.
8. Lewis Anthony Dexter, *Elite and Specialized Interviewing* (Evanston, Ill. Northwestern University Press, 1970), p. 38.
9. John T. Doby, Edward A. Suchman, John C. McKinney, Roy G. Francis, and John P. Dean, *An Introduction to Social Research* (Harrisburg, Pa.: Stackpole, 1954), p. 244.
10. Dexter, *Elite and Specialized Interviewing*, pp. 42–43.
11. Doby et al., *Introduction to Social Research*, p. 236.
12. D. H. and A. W.
13. A. W. See Hugh Heclo and Aaron Wildavsky, "Preface" to the 2d ed. of *The Private Government of Public Money* (London: Macmillan, 1981) for chapter and verse in the British Treasury.
14. Doby, p. 235.
15. A. W.
16. Gorden, *Interviewing*, p. 402; See also Doby, *Introduction to Social Research*, pp. 241–42, and Bingham, *How to Interview*.
17. Gorden, *Interviewing*, pp. 405–6.
18. Ibid., p. 406.
19. Jean Converse and Howard Schuman, *Conversations at Random* (New York: Wiley, 1974), p. 70.
20. A. W.
21. Theodore Caplow, "The Dynamics of Information Interviewing," *American Journal of Sociology* 62 (1956): 165–71, 167.
22. D. H. and A. W.
23. John T. Doby, Edward A. Suchman, John C. McKinney, Roy G. Francis, and John P. Dean, *An Introduction to Social Research* (Harrisburg, Pa.: Stackpole, 1954), p. 241; See also Gorden, *Interviewing*, pp. 402, 477.
24. Doby, *Introduction to Social Research*, pp. 241–42.
25. Lewis Anthony Dexter, *Elite and Specialized Interviewing* (Evanston, Ill.: Northwestern University Press, 1970), p. 41.
26. Doby, *Introduction to Social Research*, pp. 231–32.
27. A. W. Dexter adds that if one interviews at the top first and lower level officials know that, they may try to affirm the same story (letter to A. W.).
28. Dexter, *Elite and Specialized Interviewing*, p. 39.
29. Ibid., pp. 39–40.
30. Ibid., pp. 46–47; Bingham and Moore, *How to Interview*, p. 65.
31. Gorden, *Interviewing*, p. 249. Ted Lascher suggests interviewing congressmen in their home district offices because life is less frantic there. If economizing on time and travel does not require sticking to the place where a legislature meets, this is useful advice.
32. Dexter, *Elite and Specialized Interviewing*, p. 55. (Memorandum to Author, December 2, 1987.)

33. Theodore M. Becker and Peter R. Meyers, "Empathy and Bravado: Interviewing Reluctant Bureaucrats," *Public Opinion Quarterly* 38, no. 4 (Winter 1974–75): 605–13, 608.
34. D. H.
35. Gorden, *Interviewing*, pp. 250–51; Converse and Shuman, *Conversations*, pp. 2–3.
36. Dexter, *Elite and Specialized Interviewing*, pp. 47–48.
37. A. W.
38. Gorden, *Interviewing*, p. 251.
39. Dexter, *Elite and Specialized Interviewing*, p. 47.
40. A. W.
41. Gorden, *Interviewing*, p. 191; Becker suggests interviewing middle-management during lunchtime because supervisors tend to eat lunch at their desks and are not usually interrupted at this time. Becker and Meyers, "Empathy," p. 608.
42. D. H. and A. W.
43. A. W.
44. Williams, "Interviewing Politicians," p. 306.
45. See Gorden, *Interviewing*.
46. Doby, *Introduction to Social Research*, p. 236; Robert L. Kahn and Charles F. Cannell, *The Dynamics of Interviewing* (New York: Wiley, 1957), p. 46.
47. Caplow, "Dynamics of Information Interviewing," p. 169.
48. Kahn, p. 48.
49. Dexter, *Elite and Specialized Interviewing*, p. 49; Kahn, *Dynamics*, p. 83.
50. A. W.
51. Doby, *Introduction to Social Research*, p. 232; italics in original.
52. D. H. and A. W.
53. Doby, *Introduction to Social Research*, p. 232.
54. Gorden, *Interviewing*, p. 266.
55. Dexter, *Elite and Specialized Interviewing*, pp. 50–51.
56. A. W.
57. D. H.
58. Becker, "Empathy," p. 610.
59. D. H.
60. Becker, "Empathy," p. 610.
61. Ibid.
62. Gorden, *Interviewing*, p. 446; Converse, *Conversations*, p. 61.
63. D. H.
64. Dexter, *Interviewing and Specialized Interviewing*, p. 50.
65. A. W.
66. Gorden, *Interviewing*, p. 274.
67. Dexter, *Elite and Specialized Interviewing*, p. 59.
68. Williams, "Interviewing Politicians," p. 304; Dexter, *Elite and Specialized Interviewing*, p. 57.
69. Williams, "Interviewing Politicians," p. 304.
70. Gorden, *Interviewing*, p. 276.
71. D. H. and A. W.
72. A. W.
73. A. W.
74. A. W.

75. Dexter, *Elite and Specialized Interviewing*, pp. 57–58.
76. A. W.
77. Gorden, *Interviewing*, p. 41; see also Bingham, *How to Interview*, p. 65.
78. See, for example, Caplow, "Information Interviewing," p. 167.
79. Lewis Anthony Dexter, "Role Relationships and Conceptions of Neutrality in Interviewing," *American Journal of Sociology* 62 (1956): 153–57, 154.
80. A. W.
81. Kahn, *Dynamics*, p. 8; Bingham, *How to Interview*, p. 73; Dexter, "Role Relationships," p. 156.
82. Kahn, p. 6.
83. Converse, *Conversations*, pp. 20–21, 60.
84. Ibid., p. 18.
85. Caplow, "Dynamics," p. 170; Converse, *Conversations*, p. 51.
86. Doby, *Introduction to Social Research*, pp. 237–38; italics in original.
87. Kahn, *Dynamics*, pp. 47–48.
88. Becker, "Empathy," p. 611; Dexter, "Role Relationships," pp. 156–57; Rose, Arnold, "A Research Note on Experimentation in Interviewing," *American Journal of Sociology* 51 (1945): 143–44, 143.
89. A. W.
90. D. H.
91. Gorden, *Interviewing*, p. 346.
92. Dexter, "Role Relationships," p. 157.
93. Gorden, *Interviewing*, p. 351.
94. Kahn, *Dynamics*, pp. 11, 112.
95. Gorden, *Interviewing*, p. 41.
96. D. H.
97. Ibid.
98. Charles Morrissey, "On Oral History Interviewing," in Lewis Anthony Dexter, *Elite and Specialized Interviewing* (Evanston, Ill.: Northwestern University Press, 1970), p. 114.
99. John T. Doby, Edward A. Suchman, John C. McKinney, Roy G. Francis, and John P. Dean, *An Introduction to Social Research*, (Harrisburg, Pa.: Stackpole, 1954), p. 246; see also Bingham, *How to Interview*, p. 74.
100. Gorden, *Interviewing*, pp. 390–91.
101. Ibid., p. 340.
102. A. W.
103. Gorden, *Interviewing*, p. 467; See also S. M. Miller, "The Participant Observer and Overrapport," *American Sociological Review* 17 (1952): 97–99; and Herbert H. Hyman, William J. Cobb, Jacob J. Feldman, Clyde W. Hart, and Charles H. Stember, *Interviewing in Social Research* (Chicago: University of Chicago Press, 1954), p. 282.
104. Stephen A. Richardson, Barbara Snell Dohrenwend, and David Klein, *Interviewing: Its Forms and Functions* (New York: Basic Books, 1965), p. 202.
105. Ibid., p. 201.
106. A. W.
107. See for example Converse, *Conversations*, p. 22.
108. Morrissey, "On Oral History Interviewing," p. 113; Doby, *Introduction to Social Research*, p. 238.
109. Dexter, *Elite and Specialized Interviewing*, p. 56.
110. Caplow, "Dynamics," p. 171; Becker, "Empathy," p. 611.

111. Mark Benney and Everett C. Hughes, "Of Sociology and the Interview: Editorial Preface," *American Journal of Sociology* 62, no. 2 (September 1956): 137–42; Kahn, *Dynamics*, p. 6.
112. D. H. and A. W.; Bingham and Moore refer to the interview as "a conversation with a purpose." Bingham, *How to Interview*, p. 3.
113. Gorden, "Dimensions of the Depth Interview," p. 159.
114. Bingham, *How to Interview*, pp. 68–69.
115. Doby, *Introduction to Social Research*, p. 247.
116. Caplow, "Dynamics," p. 170.
117. Williams, "Interviewing Politicians," p. 305.
118. Converse, *Conversations*, pp. 46, 56.
119. A. W.
120. Merton and Kendall, "Focused Interview," p. 546; Gorden, *Interviewing*, pp. 122, 351–52.
121. Ibid.
122. Charles Morrissey, "On Oral History Interviewing," in Lewis Anthony Dexter, *Elites and Specialized Interviewing* (Evanston, Ill.: Northwestern University Press, 1970), p. 112; Merton and Kendall, "Focused Interview," p. 545.
123. Dexter, *Elites and Specialized Interviewing*, p. 55; see also Bingham, *How to Interview*, p. 72.
124. Richardson, *Interviewing*, p. 246.
125. A. W.
126. Morrissey, "On Oral History Interviewing," p. 113.
127. Bingham, *How to Interview*, p. 73.
128. Gorden, *Interviewing*, pp. 351–52.
129. Sidney Webb and Beatrice Webb, *Methods of Social Study* (New York: A. M. Kelly, 1932), cited in Dexter, *Elites and Specialized Interviewing*, p. 61; italics in Dexter.
130. D. H.
131. A. W.
132. Caplow, "Information Interviewing," p. 170; Merton and Kendall, "Focused Interview," p. 542.
133. Dexter, *Elite and Specialized Interviewing*, p. 62.
134. Quote from Doby, *Introduction to Social Research*, p. 243; see also Merton and Kendall, "Focused Interview," p. 554.
135. Morrissey, "On Oral History Interviewing," p. 113; italics in original.
136. Robert K. Merton and Patricia L. Kendall, "The Focused Interview," the *American Journal of Sociology* 51, no. 6 (May 1946): 541–57.
137. Doby, *Introduction to Social Research*, p. 243; Gorden, *Interviewing*, p. 138.
138. Bingham, *How to Interview*, pp. 74–75.
139. A. W.
140. Stephen A. Richardson, Barbara Snell Dohrenwend, and David Klein, *Interviewing: Its Forms and Functions* (New York: Basic Books, 1965), p. 163; Converse, *Conversations*, p. 50.
141. Gorden, *Interviewing*, p. 377.
142. Ibid., p. 434.
143. Richardson, *Interviewing*, p. 163.
144. Arnold, Rose, "A Research Note on Experimentation in Interviewing," *American Journal of Sociology* 51 (1945): 143–44.

145. Kahn, *Dynamics*, p. 207.
146. Richardson, *Interviewing*, pp. 162–63.
147. A. W.
148. Richardson, *Interviewing*, p. 161.
149. Ibid., p. 162.
150. Kahn, *Dynamics*, p. 112; Richardson, *Interviewing*, pp. 163–64.
151. Converse, *Conversations*, p. 22; Richardson, *Interviewing*, p. 165.
152. D. H.
153. Richardson, *Interviewing*, p. 242.
154. Ibid., pp. 165, 168–69.
155. Gorden, *Interviewing*, p. 439.
156. In Doby et al., *An Introduction to Social Research*, p. 245; italics in original. See also Stephen A. Richardson, Barbara Snell Dohrenwend, and David Klein, *Interviewing: Its Forms and Functions* (New York: Basic Books, 1965), p. 204.
157. Gorden, *Interviewing*, p. 377; see also Richardson, *Interviewing*, p. 204.
158. Gorden, *Interviewing*, p. 335.
159. D. H.
160. Gorden, *Interviewing*, p. 360; Richardson, *Interviewing*, p. 242.
161. Gorden, *Interviewing*, p. 360.
162. D. H.
163. Ibid.
164. Morrissey, "On Oral History Interviewing," p. 145; Merton, "The Focused Interview," p. 555. On the diverse motives of politicians, see James Payne and Oliver Wushinsky.
165. Kahn, *Dynamics*, p. 182.
166. Williams, "Interviewing Politicians," p. 311.
167. Morrissey, "On Oral History Interviewing," p. 140.
168. Doby, *Introduction to Social Research*, p. 238.
169. Ibid., p. 245; Bingham, *How to Interview*, p. 67.
170. Merton, "The Focused Interview," p. 545.
171. D. H.
172. Doby, *Introduction to Social Research*, p. 238.
173. Morrissey, "On Oral History Interviewing," p. 150; see also Bingham, *How to Interview*, p. 18.
174. Williams, "Interviewing Politicians," p. 311.
175. Ibid.; see also Gorden, *Interviewing*, p. 466; Kahn, *Dynamics*, pp. 44–45.
176. Bingham, *How to Interview*, pp. 65–66.
177. Williams, "Interviewing Politicians," p. 310.
178. Gorden, "Depth Interview," p. 161.
179. Gorden, *Interviewing*, p. 208; Williams, "Interviewing Politicians," p. 308.
180. Ibid., p. 306.
181. Bingham, *How to Interview*, p. 76.
182. Doby, *Introduction to Social Research*, p. 245; Gorden, *Interviewing*, p. 456.
183. Bingham, *How to Interview*, p. 74.
184. Dexter, *Elite and Specialized Interviewing*, p. 42.
185. Doby, *Introduction to Social Research*, p. 248.
186. Bingham, *How to Interview*, p. 69.
187. Gorden, *Interviewing*, p. 186.
188. Ibid., pp. 458–59.

189. Gorden, Raymond, "Dimensions of the Depth Interview," *American Journal of Sociology* 62, no. 2 (September 1956): 158–64.
190. Gorden, *Interviewing,* p. 268.
191. Dexter, *Elite and Specialized Interviewing,* p. 65.
192. Letter to the author, January 21, 1988.
193. Memorandum from Selma Monsky, March 9, 1988.

6

On Collaboration

Research is collaboration. The obligatory footnotes merely memorialize the fact that we are dependent on the work of others. Whether we build on or amend or oppose it, the work of predecessors and contemporaries provides the indispensible frame within which we write. The direct, formal acknowledged collaboration that is the subject of this chapter rides on the surface of indirect, informal, only partially recognized unions that necessarily undergird our efforts. Just as the monk in his cell is inescapably part of the larger society, his vocation made meaningful by his separation from life outside, so the loneliest researcher-cum-writer participates willy-nilly in the endless collaborations that constitute the traditions within which he labors. The blocks out of which our writer sculpts his material are made by his semivisible collaborators.

Collaboration as Cooperation and Manipulation

When collaboration spells cooperation, the halo cast over this enabling word lasts until it is replaced by a less sanctified description—manipulation. Yet both designations are accurate. There must be cooperation if the work is to be done expeditiously, and there must be manipulation if each collaborator is to serve the purposes of the other(s). For the ultimate rationale of a collaboration must be for participants to make use of each other's talents to do what they either could not have done at all (or as well) alone.

Since collaboration involves working with and using others (invocation of this seemingly pejorative term is, as before, deliberate), it is helpful to begin with the employment of research assistants (RAs). In that relationship both the power and knowledge asymmetries are at their greatest. Problems of abuse and incompetence, using RAs for nonprofessional work or for genuine research that makes no sense or failing to give credit where it is due, raise themselves right at the start. My own rule is that "nitwork," that is, labor not connected to the project (say, going to the post office) never take up as much as 5 percent of the total time. This formula provides a bit of flexibility for the senior researcher while assuring the junior member of an opportunity to learn about research by doing it.

Avoiding the negative, being nonexploitative, is easier than accentuating the positive, being helpful. The RA should emerge with stronger research skills and substantive understanding, and the principal investigator (as senior researchers are called by funding institutions) should be helped to further his work. Mutual gain is the common objective; the only difficulty lies in achieving it.

Apportioning the task according to the interests and capabilities of the RA is the beginning of wisdom. Though it may seem peculiar that two people will agree that one will attempt to do something for which he is unqualified and toward which he is indifferent, if not downright hostile, it happens. How? All you need do is not think about it. Just let nature take its course. Leave enough implicit, add dashes of reticence and absence, and the illogical quickly becomes the ordinary. Instead there has to be a frank interchange of views. All along the investigator should encourage the RA to reveal his interests and capabilities, presenting, if possible, several variants of the task, to the end that both parties retain their enthusiasm and optimism; realism, too. The senior party presumably has (or through experience should acquire) a sense of how much work can be done in a given period of time. Otherwise anger at being overburdened alternates with annoyance at being let down.

The kind of work to be done must, as a matter of course, vary with the needs and desires of the principal investigators. Some may be satisfied with discussing ideas or events in order to get their creative juices flowing. My preference for RAs (as for myself) is to assign responsibility for completed work, from research through writing. Then on receipt of a draft, I give specific suggestions for change, followed by revision by the RA, followed by as many iterations as it takes. Whatever the RA is capable of doing, he should do, since that enables him to learn more and the principal investigator to spend more time on the things that only he can do.

If RAs provide assistance—collecting data, interviewing, providing tables—they receive credit. If RAs write drafts, part of which remain recognizable in the final product, they receive coauthorship. (I try to follow the alphabetical rule; "try" because a publisher once insisted that my name go first, something I will not allow to happen again). The only drawback to this practice, which motivates the junior person and protects against the view that his contribution has been minimal, is that citation indexes count the first name only. Since I have yet to collaborate with Xerxes or Zimmerman, I come second, but I think it would be better for the citation indices to change their practices than for me to change mine.

The apportionment of credit may be illustrated by my collaboration with Naomi Caiden on *Planning and Budgeting in Poor Countries.* The idea came on a trip to Southeast Asia; when whiling away the time with planners and budgeters, I realized they had no real contact with one · another nor did plans become part of budgets. Perhaps I might write a new chapter on poor countries for *The Politics of the Budgetary Process.* Finding Naomi Caiden in Berkeley, I asked her to survey the literature. She turned in a draft and suggested we collaborate on a paper. By then I saw a book. A three-page proposal, sent to 50 foundations chosen from the book of foundations by Naomi, yielded a research grant. We chose three graduate students to conduct interviews in different parts of the world. Data in hand Naomi read a vast secondary literature, including United Nations reports. I reread the best pieces. She wrote chapters on planning while I did chapters on budgeting. Many, many drafts and several years later, so many I cannot now tell who wrote which paragraph, we had our draft. Then I interviewed participants in planning and budgeting in Ceylon (now Sri Lanka) and Nepal in order to determine whether we had achieved closure. The students received credit in the acknowledgments, and Naomi Caiden and I were the authors because we wrote the book.

It was different with Hugh Heclo. I encountered Hugh as a graduate student whom the political science department at Berkeley had asked me to interview in London as a prospective candidate for employment. I was impressed. Stymied in my efforts to penetrate the British Treasury, and finding that English students were too easily put off and put down by class snobbism (they could not stand being treated as idiots), I asked Hugh if he would do a few interviews. He did. The interviews were superb. On the spot I asked him if he would collaborate with me as coauthor on what became *The Private Government of Public Money.*[1]

Generosity

Collaboration among scholars of equivalent status is both similar— mutual benefit is what matters—and different. Seeing eye to eye becomes even more important. The ability to impose on each other, each doing more than half the work; the ability, if you will, to call on the generosity of one collaborator to rescue the other, can make a big difference.

When collaborators come from different fields or bring widely varying perspectives and backgrounds, much has to be done to bridge the gap. It takes time. Constant conversation is the only way (at least so it proved for me and anthropologist Mary Douglas); working at a similar pace, a compatability of metabolisms, helps. So does forbearance when what is obvious on one side is obscure on the other.

Drawing on quite different sources can be an opportunity for a richer experience, but it can also lead to mutual incomprehensibility. The antidote to that poisoning of the interdisciplinary well is not only mutual respect but also a deep-seated belief that mastering the perspective of the collaborator is meaningful. From *Risk and Culture* I gained not only a friend and a book but also an appreciation of Douglas's cultural theory that has guided my work ever since.[2] The feeling that I have gained more than I could possibly give has maintained my interest in collaboration as a vital mode of learning.

Collaboration is a two-way street; as one gains access to subjects and ideas that one would otherwise not be able to take on, his partner(s) may likewise be stimulated in new directions. When the Public Lands Law Review Commission wanted me to study budgeting in natural resource agencies, Jeanne Nienaber, now a professor, then a graduate student, asked if she could participate. In addition to the book we wrote (subtitled "Money Doesn't Grow on Trees"),[3] she has gone on to write other books on political and organizational aspects of natural resource policies. As part of a life-long practice of thinking about the ideas and organizational arrangements involved in my administrative work, I read about the history and practices of foundations involved in generating knowledge about public policy. Experience at Russell Sage Foundation led to collaboration with James Douglas on a paper about "The Knowledgeable Foundations."[4] And this collaboration in turn was indirectly responsible for his *Why Charity* (Sage, 1983). Now under a grant from this very same foundation, I am engaged with Joseph White, a graduate student in political science, on a book about *The Deficit and the Public Interest* from the last year of Carter's administration to the first six years of Reagan's. Joe is on his way to becoming one of the outstanding students of budgeting. One thing, as we say, leads to another.

Giving and Following Directions

One soon becomes aware of the difference between those who can imagine what things look like to recipients of directions and those who largely lack the capacity to put themselves in the place of others. The capacity to visualize the progression of another person's activity is crucial. Clarity of mind is even more critical in collaboration than in solo research because fitting the parts together matters more.

Knowing what you want does not necessarily, though it may, include a well–worked-out scheme. A sense of direction is sufficient. Even before Jimmy Carter received the Democratic nomination for president, for instance, I saw signs in his speeches that he had a well–worked-out but rather unusual philosophy for a political—management science. So I asked Jack Knott, then a graduate student in political science, to work with me on a paper (1) showing this was so if it were and (2) bringing out the likely consequences, mostly unfortunate, for Carter's prospects as president. The first thing was to find out if Carter's speeches, especially from his time as governor, could be obtained. They were available. Then we read them for an eyeball check of the hypothesis. So far, so good. Having gotten this far made it worthwhile for Jack to write an account of Carter's beliefs on a variety of political and administrative subjects.

This done, and thus solidified in the conviction that we were onto something important, I set about relating Carter's code of operation to common conceptions of the requirements of U.S. political life. The resulting paper,[5] which went back and forth between us many times, can stand as a retrospective as well as a prospective evaluation of the political problems of the Carter administration.

The feasibility of a collaborative effort need not be evident from the start but may emerge over time. The Oakland project, an action research project that lasted from 1966 to 1973, brought me into daily contact with graduate students and young faculty members. On trips to Washington, I was impressed with the soulful desire of public officials to know what it was really like out there in the urban boondocks. When a book appeared suggesting that minority employment had been significantly improved by a federal project, I asked Mari Malvey, a graduate student, to look at it. She wrote a paper; we all discussed it. Jeff Pressman wanted to know more, so he prepared a more substantial account. As we read it over together, it seemed to us that an awful lot of approvals by diverse agencies were required to make things happen. Therefore I asked Jeff to prepare a list and then a flow chart. That was the beginning of our study of the "Complexity of Joint Action," as the crucial chapter around which our collaboration developed was called.[6]

Collaborations can be instant. The OPEC oil price increases agitated me a great deal. I felt they were unjust; what was worse, they would have far-reaching negative consequences that experts and policymakers were playing down. By talking incessantly about the subject, I found that two friends—Paul Seabury and a visiting scholar, Edward Friedland—were similarly motivated. A quick division of labor—each one of us wanted to do and say more—was arranged. An advantage of the scholarly life is that instead of just stewing, we are sometimes able to work out what is bothering us on paper and in print.[7]

Giving direction can be sequential; each stage may reveal further possibilities. Tacit knowledge, knowing more than one can say, may come into play by reacting to unfolding events. My current project is on risk and safety. I wish to show that certain principles, such as the intertwining of good and bad effects in the same phenomena, are widespread. Following controversies about carcinogens, I became aware that several principles in which I was interested might be illustrated by the functions of the human body, for example, the immune system that is essential to health but sometimes runs amuck. Dennis Coyle, a graduate student in political science, warily accepted my challenge. I could not tell him exactly what to look for except for a few subjects and references. To have him write a draft chapter would have been a mistake. Instead he read and tried a few pages. I reread and developed rules for inclusion and exclusion; It works, I think. This week I was cheered by reading an article in the *Scientific American* that began by observing that the body's defense budget was relatively modest. If scientists can use our language, we can take a crack at theirs.

The conjunction of idea and opportunity is critical. For some time I had thought that the literatures on implementation and evaluation should be joined. Two linkages—a common concern with learning and a common urge to conceptual imperialism, making each subject into policy analysis and execution, in order to avoid rejection—suggested themselves. In order to try out these ideas however, someone industrious and with extraordinary synthetic capacity had to be found to read these burgeoning literatures and relate them. One day Angela Browne, a graduate student in the School of Social Welfare, came to ask advice about the essays she was doing as part of her preliminary examination papers. On reading her essays I knew she had the required talents. The result was the third edition of *Implementation*,[8] which I believe is far stronger in its intellectual scope than the earlier two.

Advice versus Help

In collaboration I like to distinguish between advice and help. Weak advice is telling other people what is wrong; strong advice contains suggestions for improvement, varying from the vague—would it not be nice if—to the specific—why not do it this way. I prefer help.[9] When responding to my draft, I want my collaborator to write in specific changes—additions, deletions—rather than talk about what might be done. In this way each draft incorporates the work of both authors, and each one cumulates their insights rather than their frustrations. Of course one may and should talk about what might be done, but by being required to shoulder the burden of actually doing it, an element of realism creeps in that keeps the paper or book within reasonable bounds.

A preference for help over advice also makes manageable the question of creativity. Presumably partners who collaborate have agreed on the project, a rough outline, and a division of labor. Dividing up chapters works well, but there is no reason why each author cannot do different sections of the same chapter. Creativity comes in when, during the course of research, new ideas emerge. Good. That is the way it ought to be. Yet such creativity can also be a curse by putting a strain on the partnership. Who will bring the new idea to fruition? How will it affect the general cast of the project? How long will it take? Are the collaborators in agreement? I find that by assigning responsibility for executing new ideas to the person who thinks them up, so there is a price to be paid for altering the original scheme, there are fewer such proposals, but they are likely to be more serious. Instead of remaining in the airy-fairy stage, moreover, the stipulation that new ideas be written up allows attention to be focused on the thing in itself rather than on a hypothetic notion. (The administrative version—"What do you propose to do?"—helps mightily to focus advice.) Creativity is encouraged; anything my collaborator is willing to present in the flesh, that is, on the written page, receives serious attention without leading to detours and possibly disputes about phantoms.

When I am asked how work ought to be divided in a collaboration, the questioner might think there is one best way. Not so. I have divided up the first half versus the last half, written alternating chapters, done almost the entire first draft, written different sections, and gone in between. What matters first is agreement on who should do what; second, willingness to reallocate when one cannot do what he thought he could; and third, feeling good about it. Goodwill goes a long way, though, needless to say, it cannot survive repeated failure to meet or complete assignments.

Assuming that a section or a chapter is in draft, it should become, no matter who drafted it, common property. Each time a collaborator revises a draft, the understanding is that this is the best he can do until the next time. When do the drafts stop circulating? When the best has been done that the authors can do at that time. I add the qualification of time because in line with my general incrementalist philosophy, I expect that the future will provide opportunities for new editions, not only to take advantage of new developments, but also to better approximate the original vision of what this book or article could become. Error recognition and error correction are not only themes to be urged on others but concepts I try to make live in my work.[10]

Responsiveness

Responsiveness is the key. The idea is not that two people should work as one, for then there would be little advantage, but rather that they should do better together. This togetherness requires awareness of, and responsiveness to, their differences, as well as the similarities that have led them to collaborate. Differences in style and mode of operation are as important as differences in capabilities and outlook. Perhaps an example will help illustrate what I mean.

Though we did not know it, Nelson Polsby and I began our collaboration on *Presidential Elections* by writing a graduate school paper on party reform. The desire to do a book came out of discussions when Nelson visited me at Oberlin. We agreed on a division of labor and proceeded to draft various chapters. So long as we made progress—by then I was at Resources for the Future in Washington and he was at Wesleyan—we continued working by mail, supplemented by occasional discussion by phone. Only when we had gone as far as we could apart did we work together physically.

From that day to this, my preference has been not to work in close proximity to a collaborator unless she or he already happens to be where I am. Working together to me means working on each other's work, not talking about only what we would do but mostly about what we have done. As John Wayne would undoubtedly have put it had he been a professor (do not laugh; think of Indiana Jones), the draft before us is not brag, it is fact. Otherwise I find that there is a danger of heightened anxiety (What *are* we doing?), unnecessary differences about burden sharing (What are *we* doing?), and dissipation of effort (What are we *doing*?). Getting together to discuss corrections to work in hand not only concentrates the mind (for when published, we will have to hang together) but also provides a solid platform for talking about what to do next, given that we are building on something already done.

Living in the same place, Polsby and I had to decide how and when to work together. He likes working late at night; I like the early morning. Neither of us insisted that the other write while asleep. We met at a time when we were both awake—in the afternoon. We went over each other's writing and made changes. We discussed only those changes with which we disagreed, thereby focusing attention on what needed to be ironed out.

Like another of my collaborators, Mary Douglas, Nelson has an elegant and parsimonious style; he writes "short." He is also fastidious in that, having explained something once, with economy of expression, he does not want to say it again 50 pages later. I write "long," and I tend to think that if something is worth saying, it is worth saying often, particularly if two people can say it in different ways. One mode of reconciliation is straightforward. Nelson reduces the size of my drafts, and I increase the size of his. We also tend to have somewhat different tastes in reading matter, which increases the diversity of sources on which we draw. Another mode of reconciliation is more difficult—mutual acceptance. I do what Nelson says, and he does what I say unless there are strong reasons to the contrary.

This quick account glosses over a prosaic but vital consideration: turnaround time. To work together it is essential for collaborators to keep each other going. Day-by-day, or month-by-month, they must meet their commitments to one another, for responsiveness is happiness. It would be fair to say that I was able to fit *The Politics of Mistrust*[11] into my life because of the extraordinary responsiveness of Ellen Tenenbaum, which enabled me to concentrate on what I could do best. No one, to be sure, comes through all the time. A positive sign is the production of something even if not everything, so that the process continues. Accomplishing the goal most of the time assures a steady rhythm of work that leads to a further interpenetration of minds. Mutual support feeds mutual respect.

Suppose the collaboration (or the collaborator) does not work. I recall telling a would-be collaborator, hired as a research associate, that if he devoted half the time doing work that he spent avoiding it, everything would be fine.

Feeling that the section in *Speaking Truth to Power* on craftsmanship in policy analysis was weak, I worked with a student to do better. We tried but our thoughts did not jell. One day I will go back to it and try again. In a way this paper is part of that process.

The vagaries of the human heart affect collaborations, too. One began with great promise, an extraordinarily good research design, splendid data collection, then nothing, literally nothing for 18 months. What to do? Chalk it up to experience and tell yourself not to wait so long before ending it the next time.

Motives

Like other social relationships, collaboration is a mixed-motive game. This mixture is not only inevitable, it is also, I think, desirable. Were there only a single motive—admiration, exhaustion, or distinction—it would soon wear out. One gets over being tired; one acquires necessary skills; one no sooner gains whatever advantage there is in being associated with another than it palls. It is precisely the mixture of motives, friendship intertwined with admiration bolstered by helpfulness, that enables collaboration to latch on to the different handles offered by changing circumstances so that it can grow with the times.

Motives for engaging in collaboration, in my experience, are contingent on circumstance. Aware that as dean of a school of public policy I had never done a full-scale policy analysis, I asked David Good to help me pull out all stops in an analysis of the charitable tax deduction.[12] Later it came in handy as a chapter of *Speaking Truth* exemplifying the combination of a political and economic analysis.

A lengthy and fruitful collaboration with Otto A. Davis and Michael A. H. Dempster emerged from anger and incapacity. Miffed at being denied access to the old Bureau of the Budget (BOB) (anyone who remembers that moniker now dates himself), I started playing with equations in which the BOB played a part. As far as my symbolic capacity went, I might as well have been engaged in pricking voodoo dolls as in social inquiry. Enter Toby Davis (who knew how to model a process) and his student Mike Dempster, who was willing to test the model on budget data. The earliest obstacle proved relatively easy to overcome: I taught myself calculus and they learned how to put up with my ignorance. A later problem—how to get them away from overly full schedules so our papers would get done—proved more resistant to solution. Ultimately I got them to visit me or I visited them; sequestered us away from the telephone (the inanimate enemy of this collaboration); and in a very few days, produced the drafts from which the published papers emerged. Jealousy in collaboration is less likely to be about claiming credit than about fighting relevant others—family, colleagues, students—for the time of the one wanted. Once a collaboration begins, it becomes a matter of priority and possession. Who among numerous claimants has first claim on the time and energy of one's partners in creation?

Indeed the very purpose of a project (not necessarily the only purpose but the leading one) may be to provide an occasion for collaboration. Seizing the opportunity to collaborate on studies of political culture with Michael Thompson (If you read his *Rubbish Theory*, would you not want to collaborate with its remarkable author?), he and I worked on understanding different types of poor people with David Dery, Alex Radian, and Ellen Tenenbaum. We enjoyed working together so much (the rapport, the responsiveness, the fun) that we are writing a book on *The Foundations of Cultural Theory*.[13]

Lengthy collaborations require careful nurturing. Early enthusiasm periodically has to be rekindled. Money runs out; life leads to detours. The pair collaborating are not the exact same people with the exact same interests as they were years before. It is not so remarkable that Carolyn Webber and I sustained our collaboration on *A History of Taxation and*

Expenditure in the Western World for 18 years but that we still kept our regard for one another.

Searching for Safety

The spirit of collaboration may be infectious. Certainly I have caught whatever it is. *Searching for Safety* was, in fact, inspired by a prior collaboration with Mary Douglas on *Risk and Culture*. While the earlier book dealt with the social origins of risk perception, the new work is concerned with what strategies society should follow to improve the health of its members. While writing *Risk and Culture,* I had to (compelled by my collaborator) omit interesting aspects of the debate over technological danger. While I still like that book, I felt it wrong to leave the subject by decomposing the antagonists into their social categories without confronting the issue—which sorts of actions make human life safer or more dangerous?—head on.

It took three years for me to accumulate sufficient insight to try out a different theory for increasing safety. Safety is enhanced by, I believe, confronting dangers that increase overall resource capacity in order to improve resilience, that is, by learning from adversity how to do better. Given the fiercely contested nature of this subject, I thought that to have even the slightest chance of being persuasive, the experience from which conclusions were drawn would have to surpass the ordinary. Such experiences moreover should replicate as closely as possible the world of nature, which is the ideal for human safety. If "nature knows best," as Barry Commoner once wrote,[14] I thought it time someone actually asked what nature knows or at least does.

Years before I had the good fortune to be visiting the International Institute for Applied Systems Analysis (IIASA) in Austria when ecologist C. S. "Buzz" Holling was giving a talk on the concept of resilience. Later I incorporated this concept into one of the chapters of *Searching for Safety* under the title "Anticipation versus Resilience." While preparing this chapter, I read more widely than I might have in ecological literature on animals, plants, and insects. When I came across a synoptic paper on "Surprise, Ecological Stability Theory, and a Reinterpretation of the Industrial Revolution" by Kenneth Watt and Paul Craig,[15] I was able to write a chapter on "How Nonhuman Life Forms Cope with Danger." Ostensibly the sole author, I relied on ranks of ecologists who had begun to establish principles of stability (read safety, as in persistence over time in recognizable form and function) in living things that existed, so far as known, without intention.

What then about human beings who were full of intention? After months of trying, the simplest strategy I could think of (say simple minded, if you will, for one has to own a subject before making it appear simple) was to add safety measures in order to make something as safe as possible. Making an analogy to the family car, which could hardly be started if every possible weak point were strengthened, I tried to think of an obvious area where this notion could be tested. While running a faculty seminar on risk, I was much taken by an account of the Nuclear Regulatory Commission's (NRC) safety procedures delivered by Robert Budnitz, its former head of research. After a conversation with Bob and some reading, I was amazed to discover that despite all the criticism of nuclear power safety no one had actually studied the inspectors (of pipes, welds, wiring, soil, and so on) whose job it is to improve safety.

Aside from treating inspectors like human beings who relate to each other in the classic manner of sociologists, I hoped to answer the question of whether and to what extent adding safety measures improved safety. With the aid first of the Survey Research Center and later the National Science Foundation, I asked Elizabeth Nichols, an advanced graduate student in Berkeley's sociology department to work with me on a study of inspection in nuclear power plants. Why a sociologist? Nichols understood that recreating relationships among these inspectors was essential to understanding their behavior and hence their modes of dealing with safety issues.

All the while I had been thinking about how to confront the question of naturalness. Random reading about the function of T-receptors in the immune system suggested that the human body itself was an excellent example of a natural defense system. The human body also had a quality I thought important to illustrate: Every element in life poses a potential danger, not excluding those, like the immune system, that appear devoted to safety. In this matter as in others I have just described, my main difficulty was ignorance coupled with lack of time. I wanted to write a book expressing ideas that would contribute to the debate over risk, not a lifetime occupation. Therefore as previously mentioned, I asked Dennis Coyle to investigate the defense mechanisms of the human body and, through joint discussion, to see if we could make sense out of them in terms of principles of safety.

In the same spirit, I asked Daniel Polisar, a senior at Princeton and a family friend, to study the historical development of the law of torts (personal injury) in order to determine whether this mechanism of resilience (you can sue only if you prove damage) worked better or worse than the anticipatory strategy of regulation. Torts occurred to me partly because I had long wanted to do something on law but mostly because everyone who studies risks or reads a newspaper or watches television or listens to talk shows knows that liability for injury is an important topic. Along the way I learned that legal doctrine is a marvelous tracer of changes in values. From person blame in the mid–nineteenth century (if you were cut in two, neither half could collect) to the contemporary penchant for system blame (businesses and governments pay many times more for the same injuries than do individuals), there have been vast social changes.[16]

By this time I was more than aware of how little I or any one person could know about acid rain or PCBs or asbestos or any of the myriad subjects heretofore reserved for technicians, subjects that were the everyday staple of the literature on risk. So I asked a friend, William Havender, a biochemist with an interest in social science, to read my manuscript and tell me what he thought. He had many criticisms, but basically we agreed on why public policy toward risk had gone wrong. Again I asked him to provide examples from his copious knowledge that would provide broader illustrations.

Now my four chapters of theory and principle had been supplemented by four collaborative chapters—nuclear inspection, the human body, the law of torts, reasons for going wrong. The principle subsuming the other principles of risk should now be evident: When you cannot know enough, get help. The other principle—share the blame—will not work because I am rightly too evident a target.

Collaborating with Oneself

Despite the incessant collaboration, direct or indirect, in which writers are engaged with others, their most important collaboration is with themselves. Thinking about the uses of the self helps meet the acid test of autocollaboration: Do the various strands of his work help put the diverse parts of his life together?

Teaching and research should support one another. Research should feed knowledge and enthusiasm as well as lectures and discussions about teaching. And teaching that encourages not merely elaboration but critical thought should work its way into research. Treating students as collaborators in a joint scholarly venture helps both parties learn not only about the subject matter but also about the mores of scholarly life. Attention to student writing, offering help as well as finding ''howlers,'' hones one's own sense of appropriate expression. When student papers and discussion revolve around the teacher's current research, there is mutual gain from converting enhanced interest in research into a sense of shared enterprise.

Life has its markings. Among these are requests for lectures, reviews, and papers to contribute to volumes; saying no keeps attention focused on one's main line of development. Saying yes if one is not sidetracked entirely facilitates movement into new areas that have hitherto unsuspected promise. The problem is how to fit what one wishes to do with what others wish one to do. Like Eugene O'Neill's father, who was trapped into numberless repetitions of *The Count of Monte Cristo*, early approbation can be a lifetime's snare. The trick is making creative use of these interruptions.

I am particularly fond of essay reviews as vehicles for teaching oneself about new bodies of lore. Since data are in the book or books, time spent organizing thought rather than gathering information is maximized. There is nothing wrong in using other people's effort as the occasion for an essay providing only that care is taken to do the author justice. The contents of the books should be fairly summarized and a considered judgment rendered for author and potential reader. Hopefully the opportunity for synergism provided by the format of review essays will lead to what is, in effect, another form of collaboration.[17]

Lectures can help make life whole. While young people seeking a position would be well advised to speak on a subject over which they have full control, mature scholars may wish to risk trying new themes. After all one does not have many opportunities to speak out loud about his pet subject. Verbalizing these thoughts and coping with questions are a good way of preparing for writing. From the time of preparation (when one has the audience in mind) to the actual exposition (gauging how well the ideas work) to a retrospective evaluation after the lecture is over, audience contact is also a mode of collaboration. We are professionals. It behooves us to give the audience recompense for its time and attention. Consideration of who they are, what they might want, how to get ideas across, is not far from criteria that ought to play a part as well in writing.

When asked to contribute a paper on a particular subject, I think hard about how it can be made to fit my current interests. Can it serve as all or part of a chapter in a book? Will a certain structure permit use in lectures? Can the topic be reformulated to advance thought in a direction toward which I would, in any event, wish to go? Now that my major interest is in political culture, for instance, I try to turn papers, including this chapter, into opportunities for doing just that.[18]

The danger is overreaching. The chance is worth taking however, because if successful, these detours turn out to lead further in the direction one was already moving.[19] The fragmentation of life, from which we all suffer, may be mitigated by such self-collaboration.

The center will hold if only there is one. Like the scatter diagrams of which social scientists are fond, a line may retrospectively be observed connecting the collaborations that over time impart a sense of direction to our intellectual wanderings.

Notes

Published in *PS* vol. 19, #2 (Spring 1986): 237–48.

1. For a description and analysis of how this book was written, see "Rationality in Writing: Linear and Curvilinear," chap. 2.
2. *The Nursing Father: Moses as a Political Leader* (Univ. of Alabama Press, 1984); *A History of Taxation and Expenditure in the Western World*, with Carolyn Webber (New York: Simon & Schuster, 1986); and *Dilemmas of Presidential Leadership: from Washington through Lincoln*, with Richard Ellis (New Brunswick, N.J.: Transaction, 1989) are written from a cultural standpoint.
3. *The Budgeting and Evaluation of Federal Recreation Programs* (New York: Basic Books, 1973).
4. In *The Future of Foundations* (New Rochelle, N.Y.: Change Magazine Press, 1978), pp. 10–41.
5. Jack Knott and Aaron Wildavsky, "Jimmy Carter's Theory of Governing," the *Wilson Quarterly* (Winter 1977): 49–67.
6. *Implementation*, 1st ed. (Berkeley: Univ. of California Press, 1973).
7. *The Great Detente Disaster: Oil and the Decline of American Foreign Policy* (New York: Basic Books, 1975).
8. (Berkeley: Univ. of California Press, 1984).
9. The distinction comes from Lincoln Steffens, whom I recall writing in his autobiography about the difference between turn-of-the-century reformers and politicians. When a woman's son has committed crimes galore, the boss from Boston explained, the reformers promise her justice, but the machine provides help.
10. See my *Speaking Truth to Power* (Boston: Little, Brown & Co., 1979), especially "The Self-Evaluating Organization."
11. *The Politics of Mistrust: Estimating American Oil and Gas Resources* (Beverly Hills, Calif.: Sage Publications, 1981).
12. "A Tax by Any Other Name: The Donor-Directed Automatic Percentage Contribution Bonus, a Budget Alternative for Financing Government Support of Charity," *Policy Sciences* 7 (1976): 251–79.
13. Published examples of our joint efforts are "A Poverty of Distinction: From Economic Homogeneity to Cultural Heterogeneity in the Classification of Poor People," *Policy Sciences* 19 (1986): 163–99; and "A Cultural Theory of Information Bias in Organizations," *Journal of Management Studies* 23:3 (May 1986): 273–86.
14. Barry Commoner, *The Closing Circle: Nature, Man, and Technology* (New York: Bantam Books, 1971).
15. In C. S. Holling, ed., *The Anatomy of Surprise* (New York: Wiley, forthcoming).
16. For a cultural version, see Dan Polisar and Aaron Wildavsky, "From Individual to System Blame: A Cultural Analysis of Historical Change in the Law of Torts," *Journal of Policy History* 1, no. 2 (April 1989).
17. Two early and two recent review essays may illustrate the possibilities I have in mind. See "The Political Economy of Efficiency: Cost-Benefit Analysis, Systems Analysis, and Program Budgeting," *Public Administration Review* 26, no. 4 (December 1966): 292–310; "Practical Consequences of the Theoretical Study of Defense Policy," *Public Administration Review* 25, no. 1 (March

1965): 90–103; "Keeping Kosher: The Epistemology of Tax Expenditures," *Journal of Public Policy* 5, no. 3 (1986): 413–31; a review of *The New American Dilemma: Liberal Democracy and School Desegregation* by Jennifer Hochschild, in *Constitutional Commentary* 3, no. 1 (Winter 1986): 161–73; and "The Media's 'American Egalitarians,' " *The Public Interest,* no. 88 (Summer 1987): 94–104.

18. See "A Cultural Theory of Leadership," in Bryan D. Jones, ed., *Political Leadership from Political Science Perspectives,* (Lawrence: Univ. Press of Kansas, Forthcoming, 1989). "Change in Political Culture," *Politics, Journal of the Australian Political Science Association* (essays in honor of Henry Mayer) 20, no. 2 (November 1985): 95–102.

19. To discover how a review essay on tax expenditure or a conference paper on foreign policy or a festschrift on federalism can be turned into an application of cultural theory, it is necessary to read those essays: "No War without Dictatorship, No Peace without Democracy: Foreign Policy as Domestic Politics," *Social Philosophy and Policy* 3 (Autumn 1985): 176–91; "Federalism Means Inequality," in Robert Golembiewski and Aaron Wildavsky, eds., *The Costs of Federalism* (New Brunswick, N.J.: Transaction, 1984), pp. 55–69.

Part III
THE PROFESSION

7

Teaching by Talking

Have you ever seen a man with thirty years experience come to the podium of a lecture hall with a huge manuscript, fumble through in an effort to find out where to begin, intermittently reading a few sentences, acting confused, and rummaging again? For a whole hour? Have you ever listened to a talk in which the subject, not to say the thesis, did not become apparent for thirty to forty minutes? Have you ever been part of an audience of experts told what they already knew or an audience of novices bewildered by lack of elementary explanation? Have you ever heard a joke, funny or not, only to wonder why it was in that particular presentation? The object, after all, is to inform, not merely to amuse. Have you ever been nearly (or actually) put to sleep by a voice so monotonic that it was difficult to keep track of what was actually being said?

I have witnessed all of these disasters and more. Increasingly I wonder why. How can a person live with himself who either does not prepare, thereby inviting an audience under false pretenses, or commits elementary blunders, like those suggested above, as if he had no sense of the negative effects on the assembled host? Perhaps wasting the time of others should be a misdemeanor comparable to other petty crimes. Perhaps, in a college or university, terrible talks should be considered felonies comparable to murdering the language or stealing time or kidnaping the mind.

There are, to be sure, superb speakers who manage to enthrall their audiences by an extraordinary combination of knowledge, clarity, insight, passion, and humor. Like other forms of creativity, we may never understand the sources of their genius. Curiosity has impelled me to ask several such wonders how they do it. Answers vary, of course, but every single one spoke of considerable preparation; none suggested pure spontaneity was enough. The one practice they had in common was evaluating and improving their performance.[1] At the risk of belaboring the obvious (How obvious can precepts be that are constantly violated?), I shall proceed to enumerate a number of "Do's and Don'ts" of speechmaking (as in "Don't tell jokes or stories unless they are relevant) based on a lifetime of listening to and giving talks.

Before taking the reader in this direction, I would like to begin with another consideration that everyone knows but to which, nevertheless, insufficient attention is paid—the test of a talk depends on how well it achieves its intended purpose, which cannot happen unless the message reaches the audience, which also cannot occur unless the speaker has some idea of whom she is addressing.

Purposes and Audiences:
From Student Seminars to Job Talks to Mass Lectures

I begin, advisedly, with the experience for which professors and students are jointly liable, the seminar presentation of student research papers. For the professor: *Do not allow students to read their research papers in class*. This is a deathblow to the interest of other students as the paper readers drone on interminably. Worse still, these future professors and, therefore, speakers, are socialized into the soul-deadening belief that one can go on forever, that audiences do not matter, that there is no need to fit the talk to the people out front, but that the main thing is to get to the end. The assumption is that there is no difference between a written paper meant to be read and a speech meant to be heard.

An article usually need not be read unless the reader has an interest in the subject. Even if the piece in question is assigned as required reading, it may be skimmed. Speeches, by contrast, usually have captive audiences. A decent respect for the feelings of the imprisoned is a good reason to follow this injunction: *prepare speeches as or more carefully than written material*. The difference is that while articles may begin slowly, bringing in all kinds of related but not central matters while still maintaining the interest of the reader who can decide how far she wishes to delve into the subject, the listener has no such choice to make. Advice for "speechifying" follows directly from these differences: *Do try to grab the listener's attention at the beginning of your talk*. This requires forethought. Hence *do plan your opening sequence with audience attention in mind*. There is no need to do this, of course, if your professor gives you two or three hours. Thus, *professors, do limit student presentations to ten to twenty minutes so as to compel them consciously to allocate their time. Students should learn how to give the essentials—context, thesis, competing views, evidence, conclusions—to fit the time available*. Practice makes perfect.

Because many speakers who have not yet spoken live in terror of being dumbstruck, with nothing to say, they do not realize that time flies before one has fairly begun. The real problem is not having nothing but rather having too much to say in the alloted time. Therefore, future speakers, *try out your talk in your mind or out loud with a clock present so you have a real-time gauge of length.*

Whenever I have taught large classes that include research assistants, I have had them give several lectures to the assembled hosts as part of their preparation for teaching. Using these student lecturers as a cover for going out of town is not what I have in mind. Rather, I expect to be present so as to observe the student, take notes, and make recommendations, repeating this process several times. It would be hard to justify imposing the cost of teacher preparation on our undergraduate students without an interpreting and guiding hand. Moreover, the graduate student speaker may be bewildered or depressed by the reaction to her talk. For *professors* the moral of the story is this: *Do provide opportunities for students to give lectures in classes, providing you are present to provide guidance.*

Professors and other *lecturers should practice limiting talk time,* especially in seminars. After all, the purpose of a small gathering is to facilitate interchange, not to filibuster. As a rule of thumb, *do not take more than half the available time for your talk.* It is an abuse of professorial conduct either to refuse questions (rare) or (alas quite common) wander aimlessly so no time is left.

The baptismal event for most graduate students is known in the trade as "the job talk." *Departments and research centers,* experience shows, *should make formal provision for student presentation of job talks based on their thesis.* Where such arrangements are lacking *students* should follow parallel advice: *Do make arrangements with your thesis adviser and other students to give your prototype job talk in front of an audience. Do go to each person present. Get feedback. Revise your talk.*

The usual defect is mystifying the audience about the major theme until the very end, with the result that they cannot follow the argument. An important cause of this mystification is the speaker's belief that he ought to tell his listeners about the methods he employed, his little adventures along the way, his growing realization that this is more difficult (and more important) than it seems. For good reason, there is no journal of negative results. Unless the topic itself is about methods, students should be advised: *Do not bring up methods unless you are asked to feature them.* Most of your audience is not interested. They want to make a quick estimate of the speaker's quality of mind and that can best be had by estimating the quality of the thesis and the defense of it under questioning. It may be that the applicant's written work is a better guide. Given the existing arrangements, however, impression management, limited by other people's estimates of their intellectual qualities, which cannot be managed, is the order of the day.

It is especially important for the giver to fit the job talk into time slots of varying lengths so as to teach herself how to give the gist of her presentation in smaller and smaller hunks of time. How? Practice! Whether or not one is able to give a job talk to friends and colleagues, a lot of practice is required to become fluent. Who is there to practice on? Standing still or walking (I prefer the latter), I recommend giving the talk silently under different time constraints. The silent, mental mode, however, is not for everyone (especially those who do not like talking to themselves) and, in any event, is insufficient. A mode of generating feedback is to tape one's talk and evaluate it oneself. This evaluation can be unnerving (Do I really sound like that? I wasn't aware my voice had a tendency to trail off. Could anyone make sense of these neologisms? How could I take a half hour to give a ten-minute talk?). But, if this practice is repeated, evidence of doing better should increase. In addition, one has learned a technique of self-evaluation that may be of use over a lifetime.

Sometimes the talk is given as scheduled. Other times it has to be truncated but still given in the format of a separate event. On occasion, the candidate will be sitting at lunch only to be surprised with the request that she give her talk then and there and pretty quick. Or, instead of or in addition to the job talk, there will be interviews with professors, most of whom will not have heard the talk. They are pretty sure to ask offhandedly for a summary (maybe three to five minutes) of two years of solid work. Yes, life is sometimes unfair; no, the job search is not a good time to bring this up. The ultimate justification for dancing to other people's tunes is not so much that the job talk is a rite of passage but more that the skills learned—varying the length of talks, pitching them to different audiences, grabbing audience attention while the grabbing is good—are also useful in talking and teaching.

Talking to Large Audiences in Lecture Halls

Lecturing is supposed to help educate its intended audience. Yet, in an age of tape recorders and television, one might well ask, "What is the point of continuing to use a technology older than antiquity?" Often, I must admit, there is no point. The lecture survives because so many of us have a vested interest in continuing to do what we have done before. If students can read all the lecturer has to say in a tenth of the time it takes her to say it, or listen at a more convenient time, why bother to use this superannuated form? The answer, if it is to be anything than self-justifying, must be that lecturing to large audiences adds value to learning that can be conferred only in person.

Do seek to project your excitement upon your audience so they are better able to identify with you and your subject. Those who mistakenly believe that learning is solely a cerebral matter may regard making an emotional investment as unseemly, disruptive, or, worse still, irrelevant. But those who understand better the diverse sources of human motivation, especially the capacity to organize the self to do effective work, will not slight the forces that galvanize the personality.

The large lecture hall talk is a species of another kind altogether. With hundreds of people sitting expectantly, the atmosphere is charged with theatrics. The aspiring lecturer who cannot visualize the presentation as a form of drama is ill-suited to the task. Whereas in a small class the teacher may lose contact with his students and regain it by a combination of eye contact and changed focus, large lectures are like being shot out of a cannon; once the audience is lost, waves of inattention ripple out into the cavernous hall. It is exceedingly difficult to regain contact. How to cope?

Do prepare your opening and closing lines in advance if you wish to survive the large lecture. Opening well is particularly important with a large audience. Closing is equally important not only to give the audience a restatement of the theme to take away with them but also to prevent the anticlimax that occurs when the speaker sounds like he is about to conclude only to start up again, zoom in for a landing, take off until he gives up and just stops. Knowing in advance how he is going to end gives a speaker much-needed confidence that no matter what happens he can get out of the lecture in one piece.

Is it better (or at least safer) to write out the lecture in advance? Because speakers differ so much in their styles and capabilities, no general advice can be given. But the platitude is right—*Do* (read or speak extemporaneously) *whatever you do best.* Most people, by my observation, including me, do better spontaneously, that is, without a prepared text. Like those who seek a casual, unkempt look, however, this "nothing can faze me" appearance requires a lot of prior preparation. Speakers who cannot overcome the fear of speaking in public without a prepared text should carry such a text with them. But they do not need to use the written text even though carrying one to fall back on may temporarily increase confidence. Even accomplished speakers, when lecturing on a new subject, may wish to give themselves a start from the other end: *Do carry a written version of a speech until you are confident you can carry on without one.*

If a speaker chooses to read a prepared text, he should learn how to do so while keeping his attention focused on the audience. *Do practice reading the text often enough so a bare glance will suffice for a fluid account.* And *do move about a bit.*

How animated or austere should a speaker appear? Speaking behavior should be congruent with the personality of whoever is doing the talking. However, the fact that the speaker is naturally quiet should not lead to quiescence on stage or the audience will go to sleep. On balance, *speakers should be advised to show some excitement.* For one thing, if the speaker isn't excited about her subject, why should her listeners be? For another, focusing the audience's attention on the speaker, which animation tends to do, helps sustain the unity of attention that alone can galvanize a large body of people.

Maintaining the interest of a crowd requires a highly structured format: theme, arguments for and against, illustrations, conclusion. *Do keep the speech simple and straightforward. Don't take detours; side comments are inadvisable with large audiences.* While this might be thought to be good advice in general, KISS (Keep It Simple Stupid) is especially desirable when one must move a large audience in the same direction at the same time.

Do seek empathy with your audience, even or especially if it is large. The trouble is that this advice is easy to give in general but hard to prescribe in particular. It is a little like telling another person to be funny. Some people find it hard to imagine how other people are feeling, how what they say makes others feel, and, therefore, to guide these reactions. The phenomenon of the enclosed speaker who walls himself off from his audience is reinforced by elemental fear: few people expose themselves willingly to criticism, rebuke, ridicule, or even contempt, depending on what comprises the speechmaker's worst fears. Speakers who survive their first speech should gradually become more comfortable. If they are "loose" or self-assured enough to connect up with the members of their audience, speakers may speed up or slow down or raise or lower their pitch or vary their illustrations or otherwise try to get in touch with the audience's feelings. It may help limit the damage by considering certain negative injunctions.

Don't run on and on and on and . . . . . . However spellbinding a speaker may be, diminishing returns rapidly set in. A tired audience may become a hostile audience. After all, people who have been promised relief after an hour or so may feel that their implied contract with the speaker has been violated. Even if our fictitious speaker (I am trying to avoid being sued) succeeds in sustaining his audience's interest through a second hour or longer, attention is likely to leave his teaching and move toward his self-indulgence, from the brilliance of his thought to his endurance. Of course, if the lecture is advertised as a marathon, members of the audience have to take what they get. Absent such prior notice, lecturers who demonstrate disregard for their audience should not be surprised to find their feelings reciprocated.

A common reply of lecturers who typically run on is that that is how they are. I am that awful me and "me" runs on and on. *Don't treat yourself as an object out of control,* I reply, or your audience may do the same, and they outnumber you.

There is a last chance. It is called the question period. And it just might enable the speaker to retrieve his fortunes. As the speaker intuits that (in his opinion) he has been misunderstood, he can use questions to restate the view he has held all along. *Don't complain you have been misunderstood.* There is no way to demonstrate this real or alleged misunderstanding. And the better evidence there appears to be, the closer our intrepid lecturer comes to blaming his audience. And that is not the way to make friends and influence potential clappers. Instead, *do use questions to restate your argument in a better way (if you have learned how to gauge your audience) or at least in a different way.*

Do hold something in reserve for the question period so that you, the speaker, can make your points appear fresh by delivering them in a different context. This advice may be superfluous in that the speaker may need every resource he possesses to fill an hour's lecture. The usual problem, however, is setting priorities. By the time one gets to give lectures, one ought to know enough to save a few of the best illustrations for the question period. The persuasive power of an apparently off-the-cuff response often exceeds that of the presumably prepared speech.

Do imagine questions so as to mentally prepare answers. If these questions are never asked, the intellectual exercise is still likely to be valuable. Besides, the very effort to imagine what other people might want to know is part of the act of seeking empathy with audiences previously recommended. If the questions, or some like them, are actually asked, the lecturer not only has what is hopefully an effective answer but also an opportunity to redirect the discussion.

How does the speaker deal with critical, even hostile questions? *Don't hit back; that only transfers audience sympathy back to the critic. Do disarm the critic; agree with the critic but show that the criticism only reinforces your position; explain that you have taken this criticism seriously but that it doesn't work; if you are persuaded, or think there may be merit in what the critic says, simple acknowledgment is best. If you disagree with the critic, do reply in a form most likely to allow a serious reply.*

Fortunately, lecturers are likely to know a lot more about their subjects than are members of the audience. *Do,* therefore, my suggestion is, *use your knowledge to bring your critic along.* Recently, for instance, I have undertaken the unenviable task of persuading people that damage to human life from industrial chemicals is far less than commonly thought. A questioner asks, if that is so, why is her industrial state higher than almost all others in its cancer rate? Now I know enough to ask in return: How high does your home state rank in cigarette smoking? Several members of the audience cry out, "among the highest." Q.E.D.

"Serious" and "short" are not necessarily compatible. Short and pithy answers are best both because they allow more questions (and questioners) to have their say, and because this straightforward style suggests command of the subject. I cannot swear that I always follow this good advice but I know which approach influences an audience more. Long answers, however well stated, give the audience the impression that the speaker is less interested in informing them than in calling attention to himself. Thus their verdict is more likely to be "too full of himself" rather than "too true." Just as babies are not born to be lecturers, of course, giving short answers to questions is not an inborn trait. It has to be developed by (you guessed it) practice. *Do prepare* (in your mind or on paper) *brief replies to questions you think will be asked.* And (I do not shrink from the trite if true) *do try again if at first you do not succeed in the planned spontaneity of the reply that is at once succinct and effective.*

Does all this practice seem too mechanical, too contrived? Perhaps. The alternative is a lifetime of lousy lectures. Have mercy, I say, and follow the same advice we ordinarily give to organizations and their decision makers: *Do detect and correct your errors!* Why should those of us who profess to learn for a living do less?

Whereas the applicant in a job talk should be advised *to stick to the tried and true (this is not a good time to experiment),* the more mature scholar may wish to make a different strategic decision. Speeches are a good way to try out ideas. They generate critical comments that help test whether these ideas are worth pursuing. Even more important, I think, is the socially given right to speak these thoughts out loud numerous times. For the process of preparation, delivery, and questions places thoughts firmly in the mind. Speechifying gives license to think out loud about a set of ideas, a process that, in my opinion, stimulates creativity.

Do seek opportunities to give the same talk several times, therefore, *but don't keep giving talks on the same theme.* There is a difference between stirring the creative juices and solidifying them. Eugene O'Neill's father who, having made a popular theatrical success as *The Count of Monte Cristo,* did it so often and so long that he was unable to do anything else, is a case in point. *Do not speak on a subject more than five times after you have ceased to learn more about the subject by talking about it out loud.*

I add the qualifier "twice" so as to give a little leeway for occasions when one must speak and lacks a topic or an audience is especially interested in this one. Too many exceptions, however, lead to unproductive activity so that the more one talks the less one is worth listening to. The same is true of speakers who leave their learning out of their lectures.

Do make use of historical, contemporary, and/or comparative references, both in your speech and during the question period. Because these examples change with changing scholarship, and because current events are ever new, the result is a talk that could not have been prepared much in advance and that, hopefully, will tie together past and present. An example is in order.

Suppose the subject is "The New World Order." The thesis is that the United States, facing no threat to its security other than the short-term danger of nuclear weapons left on the soil of the former Soviet Union, would seek to avoid the use of military force, preferring instead to act through multilateral institutions such as the United Nations. One can use contemporary events—the standoffishness of the United States in regard to Liberia, its readiness to leave military bases in the Philippines, its enunciation of preference in regard to Yugoslavia but its inaction compared to its United Nations-approved invasion of Somalia, together with its desire for a fast departure—to illuminate the situation. At the same time, the New World Order may profitably be contrasted to the bipolar "cold war" system and various historical balance of power systems. Along the way, the lecturer might mention some of the best literature by Arnold Wolfers, Kenneth Waltz, and the marvelous dialogue with Chou En Lai in Henry Kissinger's memoirs. It is by enriching lectures with learning, in short, that talkers live up to their moral responsibility to give the audience value added that justifies giving lectures.

The Small Seminar

Seminars are a different phenomenon altogether. There the purpose is to bring out the intellectual excellence of each student, including the professor, for a proper seminar is a common enterprise, through common examination of a body of scholarship or a set of problems, preferably both. Practices differ widely, from sharp Socratic encounters between the instructor and individual students, debates between students, reviews of literature by students, discussions of student research, and more. Obviously, the depth of penetration of the literature studied or problems analyzed accounts for a great deal. Observing masters break down a book or a field into its essential components is a rare treat as well as a standard to be emulated . . . if one can. Comparisons would be odious.

There may be a difference of opinion over whether seminars should be directed wholly to research or whether preparation for teaching should also play a significant part. The question keeps arising in the context of slighting teaching. My own belief is that, on the whole (and with notable exceptions), the best researchers make the best teachers. There is a world of difference as a teacher between the professor who writes an article for a professional journal every two or three years and the professor who does no scholarly work. The former is alive in scholarship, feeling herself to be part of a community of scholars. The latter is likely dead to the organic development and refurbished traditions that constitute learning. Thus the level of knowledge and consideration of new questions are likely to be much greater among teachers who are also scholars.

Professors, do write research papers together with your students. There is no better way of learning what it takes than working with someone who knows. Precisely because instructions to be creative are vacuous and no one understands how creativity occurs, so no one can give direct instructions, working with a master is the best way to learn an art and craft. An earlier paper, "On Collaboration," contains the rules I have found most useful in conducting joint research, including research with students. Here I wish to add that a seminar for graduate students is the ideal place for them to learn how to write a professional, that is, peer-reviewed, publishable research paper. Here I have inclinations but not necessarily directives. Given a choice, I am not in favor of a doctoral seminar organized solely around each student's dissertation. My reason is that the subject matter is usually so disparate that the seminar lacks cohesion. The "nuts and bolts" of thesis preparation tend to drive out discussion of ideas. Besides, no one, including the instructor, knows enough about such a disparate array of subjects to provide effective guidance.

Seminars on specific subjects offer an opportunity for graduate students to be taught to write research papers. Besides the obligatory and desirable literature review—it is a scholarly obligation to acquaint students with the literature in their chosen fields—I have found certain practices useful. One is to devote the second semester of a seminar to revising a paper the student has written in the first semester. Instead of regarding papers as classroom exercises, students are encouraged to write them to professional standards. Assuming the necessary evidence is in the paper, we go over each part of the paper—how to open and how to close—separately, several times if necessary.

Apprenticeship

Research on scientists by Harriet Zuckerman, among others, shows that the surest path to becoming a Nobel Prize winner is to work with one.

More and more, I am of the opinion that the best way to teach and to learn is apprenticeship.

For researchers the thing to *do* is to *work with students as co-investigators*. Participating in research, by doing part of the work, is desirable; participating by being one of those responsible is even better. Which is to say that there is no better way to prepare to do research and to write research papers than by viewing the task realistically as if one (in this case, the aspiring student researcher) were responsible for the final product.

If, indeed, as I believe, research requires an appropriate mental set, then the task of the experienced partner is more than dividing up the work. The experienced partner should *let research apprentices in on the critical, strategic choices. Do discuss why this particular piece of research is being conducted by explaining how it fits into the larger picture of accumulating knowledge.* It is exactly this sort of understanding and insight that is lacking from formal instruction. Consequently, much that happens appears to be uncaused. Since the advantage of apprenticeship is observing how work is done, adding the "why" by discussing the decisions made along the way adds measurably to the instruction-by-observation.

Do, especially, I would urge master researchers, *explain to your research assistants why you believe the cutting edge of your field requires a certain kind of research.* It is this insight that, when on track, enables apprentice researchers to move up and become intellectual leaders on their own.

When it becomes time to present research papers, the tendency is to let the "big guns" do it.[2] This tendency is strengthened by concern that the top people might be seen to be ducking criticism. Nevertheless, without suggesting what would be appropriate for every occasion, I would end this paper with a final suggestion: *Do allow and encourage younger researchers to do their share of countering criticism by answering questions at meetings and responding to written criticism.* The fun and the anguish go together.

Appendix:
Advice for Teaching by Talking

For Professors Who Are Both Teachers and Researchers

- Do not allow students to read their research papers in class.
- Do limit student presentations to ten to twenty minutes so as to compel them consciously to allocate their time.

- Do provide opportunities for students to give lectures in classes, providing that you are present to provide guidance.
- Do practice limiting talk time.
- Don't ignore preparation for seminars on the ground that this is not necessary.
- Do invest seminars with energy.
- Do seek opportunities to give the same talk several times but don't keep giving talks on the same theme.
- Do not take more than half the available time for your talk.
- Do not speak on a subject more than five times after you have ceased to learn more about the subject by talking about it out loud.
- Do explain to your research assistants why you believe the cutting edge of your field requires a certain kind of research.
- Do work with students as co-investigators.
- Do write reseach papers together with your students.
- Do let research apprentices in on the critical, strategic choices. Do discuss why this particular piece of research is being conducted by explaining how it fits into the larger picture of accumulating knowledge.
- Do allow and encourage younger researchers to do their share of countering criticism by answering questions at meetings and responding to written criticism.

For Students Preparing a Job Talk

- Departments and research centers should make formal provision for student presentation of job talks based on their thesis.
- Do make arrangements with your thesis adviser and other students to give your prototype job talk in front of an audience. Do go to each person present. Get feedback. Revise your talk.
- Learn how to fit the essentials—context, thesis, competing views, evidence, conclusions—into the time available.
- Stick to the tried and true (this is not a good time to experiment).
- Do not bring up methods unless you are asked to feature them.

For All Who Speak in Public

- Try out your talk in your mind or out loud with a clock present so you have a real-time gauge of length.
- Do what you do best.
- Do carry a written version of a speech until you are confident you can carry on without one.

- Do prepare your opening and closing lines in advance if you wish to survive the large lecture.
- Do practice reading the text often enough so a bare glance will suffice for a fluid account. Do move about a bit.
- Do seek empathy with your audience, even or especially if it is large.
- Don't treat yourself as an object out of control.
- Do detect and correct your errors.
- Don't complain you have been misunderstood.
- Don't run on and on and on and . . .
- Do seek to project your excitement and the importance you attach to your subject upon your audience so they are better able to identify with you and it.
- Do try to grab the listener's attention at the beginning of your talk. Do plan your opening sequence with audience attention in mind.
- Do keep the speech simple and straightforward. Don't take detours; side comments are inadvisable with large audiences.
- Do make use of historical, contemporary, and/or comparative references, both in your speech and during the question period.
- Do imagine questions so as to mentally prepare answers.
- Do prepare brief replies to questions you think will be asked.
- Do hold something in reserve for the question period.
- Do try again and again if at first you do not succeed in the planned spontaneity of the reply that is at once succinct and effective.
- Don't hit back; that only transfers audience sympathy back to the critic. Do disarm the critic; agree with the critic but show that the criticism only reinforces your position; explain that you have taken this criticism seriously but that it doesn't work; if you are persuaded, or think there may be merit in what the critic says, simple acknowledgment is best. If you disagree with the critic, do reply in a form most likely to allow a serious reply.
- Use your knowledge to bring your critic along.
- Do use questions to restate your arguments in a better (if you have learned how to gauge your audience) or at least in a different way.

Notes

1. As best as I can calculate over many years, I have talked to around fifteen superlative speakers about their craft.
2. It has become traditional for scientists in charge of laboratories to sign their names to research whether they had any part in the work or not. Perhaps the historical rationale for this practice was once defensible. Now I think it lacks an acceptable rationale.

8

On Being a Department Chair

Just as Harry Truman advised public officials who wanted to be loved to buy a dog, so faculty members who wish to be rewarded for their service as department chairs should buy savings bonds if they want a sure return. It is wiser to assume that the rewards, if any, are to be found in the next world. When you, as chair, start feeling that you are underappreciated, that you give so much yet get so little, it is time to quit. At an institution that values scholarship, the best you can hope for is for your colleagues to wait a few months before being asked, ever more insistently, "But what have you done lately?"

What should a departmental chair do? Why, he or she should serve the department interest. In the following section I shall try to add content to that elusive but nevertheless indispensible concept. Then I shall delineate some of the ways in which the departmental interest may be manifested in ordinary administration, political administration, and super-crisis.

The Departmental Interest

The departmental interest requires that faculty members not look at the chairmanship as something to be sought but rather as a duty to be endured. Were the chairmanship a desired objective, numerous evils would follow. Politicking would become more important than innovating, administration (where experience would count toward a chairmanship) more important than scholarship. If a chair is so all-fired wonderful, scholarship that leads to publication and teaching can't be so important. This decline in the importance of scholarship would be reinforced because, on average, as administration became an avenue of advancement, chairs would be less capable scholars. Whereas in the arts or sports less capable artists or players may make splendid critics or managers, the same is not true for scholarship. Among scholars, my strong impression is that "it takes one to know one."

If it is not scholarship nor monetary reward that matters (chairmanships typically bring in only a few thousand more a year, discounted by lack of time to engage in other money-making pursuits, such as consulting or summer teaching), what does? Exercising power. How? By intruding the chairmanship into all sorts of matters once considered routine. Department members may gradually come to believe that they owe what they get to this seemingly indispensable intermediary. An indirect way of accomplishing the same thing is to intrude the higher reaches of the university bureaucracy into department affairs. All of a sudden, the deans or provosts or vice chancellors are in on everything. Nothing apparently can be done without them. Instead of the intellectual exploits of its faculty and students, department stories now revolve around the idiosyncracies of provost X or dean Y who, one is assured, is on the department's side or would be so inclined were it not for a mysterious factor that can be guessed at but not known except (you guessed it) for the good offices of our indispensable intermediary, the department chair.

As a result of these machinations, that essential quality, the department interest, gets lost from departmental deliberations. Now that the department has been reduced to a cog in campus-wide plans, always assumed to be operative but actually enveloped in fog, there is no place for what, through curriculum and personnel changes, should be the strengthening of shared norms around what constitutes excellence. Moreover, there is an unfortunate displacement of roles. Higher administrators need to understand what each department wants in view of its own conception of its interests. Instead it gets a sense of what the chair thinks the dean or provost wants. Thus even the higher-level administrators are deprived of information on preferences essential to their tasks.

For department chairs to pursue the departmental interest they must know what that is and expound it to their colleagues. As always, rhetoric matters, especially if it is accompanied by congruent actions. To the extent that such a collective interest has not yet been discovered or articulated, it is the chair's task to do so. The most important departmental interest is a shared sense of excellence in research and teaching. Easier said than done, nurturing that sense of common purpose in general declarations, though that might create more trouble than it would get rid of, is the least of it. Discussions with colleagues, first privately at length, and several times, if necessary, about appointments and promotions and the admission, retention, and placement of students, are the way to create (or make explicit the existence of) shared understandings about the quality and quantity of scholarly work required of faculty and students. Case law becomes common law to be acknowledged as a departmental standard that can be invoked against more partial interests, such as personal friendship or subfield preference or trades among fields so each can get its preferred candidate. It matters that members evoke a departmental interest even if there are differences over what it signifies in a particular instance.

A departmental interest includes staff and students as well as faculty. Indeed, because faculty have higher status and are in a position of some power in regard to students, the chair should be alert to prospects of abuse. Of course, it works both ways. The protections now given staff through union agreements and administrative arrangements make it difficult to dismiss anyone, even when their performance is awful. The record-keeping burden alone is substantial. Yet one or two employees who either do not work or do poor work can demoralize an entire department. By the same token, a chair wants to show appreciation for good work and take account of employee problems. In large departments there may be an administrative assistant or an associate chair who is in the first line of supervision in regard to staff. Then these tasks may be delegated. However, I would not feel satisfied without at least a conversation a semester with each and every staff member. Heading off problems, as we all know, is a lot easier than solving them.

Since the right of the chair to talk to faculty is one of his most important assets, using that right to help colleagues, without any other matter at stake, helps build a reservoir of support that extends to other things.

I am not one of those who believe that people who spend a lifetime in a field without writing about it for their colleagues are likely to be superior teachers. Quite the contrary; those who know the most are, on average, in my experience, the best teachers. But some are not. The first thing a chair needs to do is find out about teaching. Fortunately, there are more systematic efforts to collect student appraisals than existed when I was a chair in the 1960s. These should not merely be collected but looked at and, if necessary, discussed with the professor. A chair may have developed some ideas about how to improve teaching, no doubt all of them, as in my experience, labor intensive. Or colleagues the chair knows who care about and are good at teaching may be put in touch with one who is less able in this respect, all, of course, with mutual consent. And there are now services on campus aimed at helping individuals improve their teaching. These tutoring and learning services for students are extremely valuable but are often ignored as they are not part of the academic structure. A little effort at communication, so professors know whom to call about what, helps a lot. I like to give students a specific name and phone number to call rather than a general admonition to seek help.

The requirement that teaching appraisals be included in discussions of promotions and merit increases is a good one. When teaching performance is poor and remedial efforts fail, the individual may still be valuable to the institution for administrative skills or extraordinary scholarship. If that is so, the chair should talk with deans or provosts as well as the individual involved and arrange a schedule, kinder to students, that will enable the professor to do more of what he is good at and less of what is painful for others. Should there be insufficient offsetting virtues, I would not approve tenure or promotion or a merit increase. (Correspondingly, the occasional colleague whose scholarship is a bit lacking, good perhaps but not quite good enough, should be supported for tenure and promotion if that colleague has extraordinary teaching ability. Good institutions are known in part by their flexibility.)

The general rule must be that students matter greatly and therefore that teaching matters. I confess to still liking it. But I have come to realize that some faculty, especially as they grow older, no longer like to teach undergraduates and some do not like to teach at all. These cases have to be dealt with on an individual basis, largely, I think, by creating other ways in which faculty can contribute to the common weal. A chair should be especially sensitive to colleagues who have been administrators or who have had positions that give them, say, a couple of years leave or a number of years at half-time, because, after such experience, it becomes difficult for some professors to imagine themselves going through the teaching cycle, whether it is lectures or grading papers or advising. These professors have to be gently but firmly reminded that teaching is their responsibility.

Recall the admonition against expecting rewards. Following one of the precepts outlined above, I interviewed a distinguished elderly colleague during my first few weeks and got very little from him except a pervasive dissatisfaction, one might even say alienation from the department. Looking back over his records, I discovered that he was eligible for and should probably have received a number of salary increases. After consulting with the dean, who heartily agreed, we figured that about a $6,000 increase would set things straight (multiply at least by three to get the current value), and he took the matter to the Budget Committee, the Berkeley Faculty personnel committee. I called Professor X in, told him that in view of his distinguished contributions, the University had decided he deserved an unsolicited increase of some $6,000 plus a year. He glowered, though I did not expect at all what came next: "Is it retroactive?" Nonplussed, having only been on the job a few months, I stammered out that I might be mistaken but I thought that, as with all such matters, the increase would take place at the beginning of the fiscal year, only several months away. "Fuck it," he said, "then I don't want it!" and stomped out of the chair's room where he had been so rudely insulted. Nevertheless, I believe he cashed his checks.

It is well known that internal conflict is a besetting vice of academic departments. Quarrels are easy to begin and seemingly impossible to end. Once started, internal divisions can pesist for decades, carrying their animus long after the originators have departed the scene. Working out conflicts before they have an opportunity to fester, therefore, is a major task of a chair. In my experience, departmental conflicts have come from three sources—ordinary administration, political administration, and super crises—continuing and spectacular and small and sometimes amusing and otherwise dreary. I shall try to separate these sources of conflict and discuss how a chair might deal with them.

Ordinary Administration

Ordinary chairs in ordinary times should remember the rule—have fun while you're doing it because there won't be any afterward. No one will remember, no one will care, and no one will remind you except to take note of that hole in your vita. The best thing I did before becoming chair (the graduate dean was then administering the department and not enjoying it) was to insist on having a genuine department administrator to take care of the forty-plus professors and associated staff. I thought this was farsighted, not knowing that campus administration was thinking seriously about it and that, therefore, I was knocking on an open door. LeRoy Graymer proved a godsend. But not right away. He had to learn the ropes and I had to learn how to make my colleagues appreciate the value of an administrator and simultaneously relieve my burdens by going to him with a variety of problems. Naturally, they thought it better to call me all hours of the day and night. Over time, however, as they began to see how well they were being served, and how much trust the associate chair merited and had placed in him by the chair, this changed. Having a talented associate chair who was not only a splendid administrator but full of ideas on how to improve administration, and not a slouch at department policy either, albeit in muted tones, made a huge difference. The health of the chair should matter too.

Over time, Associate Chair Graymer took from me the chore of preparing the department budget. There was an awful lot to know, but not about allocating resources. That was impossible under the system that prevailed then and, so far as I know, prevails now. The $1 million-plus department budget was mostly taken up with salaries that were decided mostly by the budget committee, upon the recommendation of the administration. My requests as chair and later as dean that we be given lump sums so that we could distribute merit increases and do something to earn our salary were uniformly rejected. This meant that no request took away from any other request. And this is not resource allocation. Such practices solidify the identity of chairs as trade unionists for professors. The department received $25,000 or so from a special fund, which was the object of considerable attention, because it was all we had to allocate as we chose. Still, when questions came up of transfers between funds, of whether a talented employee could be paid more under one label or another, Graymer came either to know it all or to know who knew it all, and so prospered.

By the second week of my chairmanship, I knew that the new administrative assistant was not capable of doing her job. She had to be replaced. Yet, before this, I had never hired let alone fired anyone. For three days I agonized over this decision, more time than I have taken on any remotely comparable matter since. And, generally, without distress. Eventually I decided that firing people was part of the job and if I could not do that I had to give way to someone who could. That makes it sound too crude. Talking to the employee in question as much as I could, I realized that much more was going on than was showing on the job. So, with her consent, I called in psychological counseling. Within a few days a change was made helpful to the employee and the department. After a period of rest and rehabilitation, I understand, she performed well in a higher level but quite different kind of job.

No one is more important to a chair than his secretary. He or she (I have hired secretaries of both genders) expedites the tasks to be performed and, if I have my way, checks on their implementation. I had my department secretaries prepare lists of items to be implemented. They checked progress and let me know if the item wasn't moving. More important, I tried to imbue the secretarial-cum-administrative staff, including undergraduate and graduate secretaries, with a sense of departmental objectives so they might see themselves as serving a larger purpose. An effective way to do this is to inform staff of important departmental decisions on curriculum, personnel, and campus-wide issues. If the staff has a sense of mission, they help communicate it to students and faculty as well.

I have been fortunate in finding marvelously capable people who have been of enormous help. Once, however, in a research capacity, I hired a secretary who might charitably be described as hostile-dependent. This secretary both wanted direction and resisted it so that the poor chair was left exhausted while being complained to about overwork. Every time I think of the difference between that situation and the others I have had, I breathe a great sigh of relief.

One of a chair's most important tasks is its institutional development. By that I don't mean growing larger; rather, I mean developing the capacities of the people who work with you and the organization to which you all contribute. (In recent years, given my interest in budgeting, I have been dismayed to see how little attention directors of the budget pay to the Office of Management and Budget itself.) A good administrator should leave behind not only effective policy but people and organizations that are more capable than the one he inherited. And that means nurturing ability wherever it is found.

The first thing to do is to take an interest in where your employees come from and where they want to go and how they might get there. It means, secondly, gradually increasing the range and scope of responsibility so that personnel grow by doing different things and taking more responsibility for them. If there is anything I hate in an organization it is people who hide in the division of labor, who say "I did my job," as if carrying a message between C and D, without seeing that it got to its destination or had the intended effect, was doing one's job. Everyone has to be motivated to do completed work, that is, to take on the organization's task as their own. If that proves impossible, serious consideration should be given to letting the employee go. On the one hand, premature enlargement of tasks may make the person involved fearful; on the other hand, never advancing responsibilities leaves them stale and without a mechanism of determining what they can do. I prefer to err on the side of more rather than less. Satisfaction comes in observing the people you work with enlarging their capacities. Leaving a stronger staff for your successors is part of serving the departmental interest.

Political Administration

Professors are born rationalizers. They are gifted at taking, defending, and abandoning positions one after another. Treating departmental decision making as if it were a matter of intellect, therefore, is a losing game for the chair. Who can outsmart so many gifted people? And who would be foolish enough to try? But there is a difference between being intellectually smart and being politically wise. In academic departments, wisdom means managing conflict. My suggestions follow.

Talk to your colleagues and keep talking. In a fundamentally egalitarian departmental structure, chairs have little authority, but the right to talk is one of them and should be exploited to the full. In addition to the other benefits flowing from this practice, a chair who listens can find out how colleagues are likely to vote on contested items before the vote takes place.

There are enough meetings. I learned not to call meetings unless there was (a) something specific that needed to be decided and (b) something on which the faculty agreed or could be persuaded to agree. I liked to do my persuading before and not during the meetings. Quarrels begun or carried on in meetings can last a long time. And I did like to know how the meeting was going to come out before I entered. What is amazing is how little this sort of elementary political calculation goes on in political science departments.

A department chair should never assume his colleagues have been treated fairly or even that ordinary administrative matters have been completed. Every colleague should be interviewed and asked specifically whether he or she is happy with the way things are going. Even that approach, however, is too general. There should be questions about pensions, benefits, leaves, salary, teaching and the sense of being appreciated. I began this practice at Berkeley, my entire administrative experience then consisting of one year's membership on the graduate committee, because that was what the party workers did with whom I intervened on behalf of my immigrant father in the 1930s and 1940s. From this I heard detailed tales of woe, almost all of which, if noted, were easy to take care of. This colleague feels slighted because she has not been put in for a teaching award and another feels that his sabbatical credits are too few. A third colleague feels that his work is underappreciated, a feeling that is not easy to alter but not impossible to work on.

The chair, if he has not already done so, should read the work of colleagues when they come up for promotion and render a judgment. He should also talk to others in the field. Maybe there is nothing to be done as the judgment is deserved. If there is a discrepancy between the worth of the work and the feeling of being honored for it, then a chair can get other colleagues to motivate disciplinary awards, papers at conferences, even a kind word now and again. Large universities tend to be cold places. Arranging celebratory occasions is a pleasant and useful activity for a chair.

Great universities are bottom heavy; the important decisions that establish their character—the capability of faculty and students, the suitability of the curriculum—should be made at this organizational level. For there, if anywhere, is the repository of knowledge and learned intuition of what constitutes excellence in each field. Higher level bodies cannot possibly know or sense or care as much about intellectual quality. Indeed, when a field of study is a collection of traditions, as in political science, the subfields may well be the proper repositories of decision. That is why the judgment of a chair, either in choosing the best faculty or in knowing who is best able to choose, is vital. That is why when one hears that provosts and presidents are the main movers, there is reason for concern. Dealing with external bodies, considering the surrounding community, occasionally (very occasionally) intervening to provide new deans and chairs when the departments or schools in question have failed to function properly, by all means, but not continuous direction of departments.[1] Departmental, that is, faculty, failure to keep up with or lead its field and to instruct its students so they receive appropriate appointments can be remedied only at higher organizational levels.

It would be absurd and counterproductive for a chair to conceive of herself or himself as the parent, the combined mother-father of the department. It is absurd because departments are usually egalitarian, at least among the full and associate professors, or oligarchic, rarely hierarchical. Willingness to subordinate one's views is at a minimum, the capacity to express them forcefully at a maximum. The young may know more than the old, possess superior skills, and have mentors elsewhere who can challenge overly demanding senior faculty. All are, after all, professors. When colleagues see their concerns met in small matters, they are more likely to accept the chair's authority in larger concerns.

I love surprises, but not at department meetings. A chair who calls a meeting without knowing what he wants is asking for trouble. A chair who doesn't know how a meeting will turn out is not doing his job. If a chair doesn't have a good idea of where his department should go, he should let someone who does do the job. A chair is much more likely to keep his department cohesive and imbued with a sense of purpose if he arranges meetings to express the agreements that exist, while keeping disagreements out of public sight. These should be taken up face-to-face, one-on-one, to preserve hard-won civility. To be more precise, deliberate meetings are useful when there is widespread agreement on the general direction the department ought to go but a lack of appropriate instruments of policy. Disagreements over direction, by contrast, are likely to create or exacerbate hostility unless guided by understandings that all are searching for the departmental interest. Throwing one's weight around would be counterproductive because it encourages rebellion.

It is appropriate, however, for chairs to take on a nurturing role. There is never enough effort to build the capabilities and careers of all concerned. Unless such overtures are rebuffed, chairs should see to it that senior faculty who are willing (or they themselves) try to develop available talent.

A department chair performs a political function—motivational maintenance and institutional change. Whether one is amazed that anything coheres or that change occurs so slowly, maintaining support from diverse constituencies—faculty, students, department staff, campus administrators, the profession at large—is essential. Leadership requires the usual qualities—energy, decisiveness, vision. In one sense, however, universities are different. The rhetoric is more high flown but the motives are more transparent. And this transparency is never more evident than during crises.

Being A Chair During the Free Speech Movement (FSM) at Berkeley

For the three years I was chair of the political science department of the University of California at Berkeley, from July 1966 through June 1969, the leitmotif was a kind of inspired madness. It was the simultaneity of crises that made these events either awful or wonderful depending on one's taste for the histrionic.

One of my very few regrets about academic life is that I did not think then to keep a diary. Whereas being a dean of a school of public policy later was relatively calm and quiet so I could remember the key episodes when I wanted to write about them,[2] there is no way now that I can recreate as well as a diary could the multiple happenings, each one bizarre enough in and of itself, no less the interaction among them.

When teaching at Oberlin in 1958 to 1962, the only other regular academic job I have had, I liked everything about it except for the incessant discussion of students, sometimes extending to their private lives. The free-speech movement at Berkeley converted it from a cosmopolitan to a local place in which "the students" were an endless and, for me, not that fascinating, source of discussion. Like everybody else, I found myself enveloped in endless meetings about the occupation of this building or that or of the chancellor's office, about whether students should be allowed to cheer and jeer at faculty meetings, about what rules were or were not appropriate for free speech, whether rules about time, place, and manner of holding discussions outside of class were subject to regulation or were not. On and on and on. Never shall I forget the meeting at Pauley Ballroom, with over a thousand faculty, or so it seemed to me, when a distinguished professor, whose work I admired greatly, asked, with rhetorical flourish, what our students meant when they kept telling us to engage in self-procreation. By then, I thought I knew.

My personal problem, albeit one widely shared, was how to maintain the scholarly work that I had come to Berkeley to pursue. This was the only time in my life as an adult I can remember not being engaged in research. Then, an intersection of two things came to my aid. I had begun The Oakland Project, devoted to action research, in which I supervised a number of students who provided assistance to the mayor, the city manager, the city council, poverty program activists, and others in the city of Oakland, and from which these students and I eventually wrote books about the fascinating city in which I have lived now for twenty years. The point here is that these students were committed to their work and therefore did not ask foolish questions like whether studying statistics would warp their minds. Fortunately for me, I was not in the position of regarding "these students" as an enemy, a foreign force to be warded off. That would indeed make a mockery out of being a teacher.

After a while, as I struggled to get more time to work, a valuable thought suddenly came to mind. Our student radicals were late sleepers; indeed, nothing much happened until about 11:30 a.m. Thus I began coming in earlier and earlier, discovering that if I started around 7 or 7:30 and kept going until 11:30, that was about as much scholarly work as I could do in a day. It also meant that I could let the free speech movement roll over me in the late mornings and afternoons and evenings without feeling that I had given up an important part of my life's purpose. And good humor was certainly essential for survival.

One morning, encountering a well-known professor in the offices of the political science department, I went to greet him only to discover five or six students, all male, all in various stages of undress, racing around him crying that he had sold out, I couldn't tell to whom or what for. Nor did anybody turn a hair, considering such events to be standard. Another day I saw riots in the making and dashed up, together with my friend Peter Sperlich, to talk to the police and administrators in front of Sproul Hall where our presence may or may not have ameliorated the situation; at least nobody got beaten. By that time, I had understood that throwing students in the way of police was a major method of radicalizing them and perhaps the major purpose behind these events.

That was only in the morning. In the afternoon there would be petitions from graduate students, who were teaching assistants, asking that they be excused from giving class because FSM thought that it was a good idea to add complaints from students that their education was being ruined to requests that the violations of university rules not be held against students who were working for degrees. The last was an easy one since all of us wanted to keep academic life separate from political life. But there was the rub; they kept intersecting no matter which way we went.

A major task of my chairmanship was to keep the turmoil on the outside from destroying colleagiality inside the department. So I went to considerable lengths to show that all members received even-handed treatment, no matter which side they were on and whether or not they agreed with my increasing opposition to these goings on. If in doubt, I always resolved it in favor of colleagues who supported FSM.

A stroke of good fortune was my growing friendship with a man whose qualities I admired perhaps more than any before or since, Jacobus tenBrook, a scholar who was blind and, among other things, did great work on laws affecting poor people and on the *Anti-Slavery Origins of the*

Fourteenth Amendment. In addition, he was a great expert on free speech, knowing what it did and did not require, and was known for his brilliant use of the Socratic method. When you got an argument past "Chick" tenBrook, nothing could touch you. It was his guidance I sought and followed at every turn, thinking, correctly, that he was not only smarter but wiser on this matter than I. There follows a typical episode whose irony has facilitated my otherwise faulty memory.

Besieged as usual, called to act upon vandalism in which several students overturned filing cabinets, strewing out their contents in Sproul Hall, the chancellor's office issued a statement to the effect that these students would be suspended, unless of course their department chairs certified that they were indispensable to the teaching program. Now wait a minute. If I am going to immolate myself, I like to be asked first. All of a sudden, therefore, I had to decide which way I would rule. Immediately I sought out Chick tenBrook to see if my initial thoughts would pass muster. However difficult the discussion, I knew I would have a fine time as Chick always mixed hilarity with help.

Shortly thereafter a graduate student under provisional suspension came to see me. He came to talk to me man-to-man, as he put it, so that he could make plans for his future life in case he were expelled. He would not tell me how to decide, though of course he wanted to stay on and serve his students, but he did require a rapid decision, meaning no longer than two days. I would rather have waited a few more days to ruminate on this matter, but, in view of the student's heartfelt plea, and the fact that I had already consulted tenBrook and knew where I would come out, I agreed to his request. Two or three days later my recommendation was published, including its reasoning, which held that a teaching assistant owed more not less fidelity to the institution and that he, not campus rules, was responsible for whatever disruption occurred in the lives of his students. That same day or perhaps the day after a leaflet appeared in which "Chairman Wildavsky" was accused of various misdeeds, a leaflet I had reason to believe the young man had helped in preparing, in which the worst thing about my action was not the decision itself but the unseemly haste in which it was issued.

Those were the days when one did not have to think about where to entertain guests; all that was necessary was to take them to witness the occupation of Moses Hall or some other such place. Though mechanisms for communication to and within the faculty had been improved, no one felt well-informed, everyone wanted to know what was happening, and no one claimed to know. So it is time to stop the atmospherics and get on to how a chair might handle such an extraordinary series of situations. Allowing them to express themselves, deflecting their reactions one way or another, letting them know their thoughts were known and that the chair was interested in them, did more to defuse the situation than any specific action. Good personal relations help smooth over other difficulties.

What proved to be impossible, at least for me, was keeping departmental conflicts wholly apart from campus-wide disputes. These events taught me the importance of cross-cutting cleavages. I worked hard to resolve or paper-over conflicts of many years' standing. Older faculty members were given recognition but not power, middle-aged members were given power but not so much recognition, and younger ones were saved from being pulled apart by the contending currents. When the same people who differed in the department also turned out to differ on questions involving the free speech movement, however, all the work done one day would be undone the next. The cost was the departure of two distinguished political theorists, a great loss, which I counted then and count now as a failure. The chair's job is to add intellectual distinction to a department, not take it away.

Who could enjoy such a situation? I enjoyed the pace, the fire-fighting, the unexpected, the necessity of devising different formulas for different occasions and types of problems, the hurly-burly, even the idiocy of much that went on. Maybe it takes one to love one. I took pleasure in the constancy of crises, sometimes two and three times a day—an appointment in danger because the candidate worried about living amidst fear of tear gas on campus, another building occupied: Should the police be called? Should classes be held under this or that circumstance?—which made the theater of the absurd appear like an exercise in normalcy.

Notes

1. Martin Trow, "Leadership and Organization; The Case of Biology at Berkeley," Chapter 7 in Rune Premfors, ed., *Higher Education Organizations: Conditions for Policy Implementation* (Stockholm: Almqvist and Wiksell, 1984).
2. See Aaron Wildavsky, "Appendix" to *Speaking Truth to Power* (Little, Brown, 1979).

9

Why It Is Necessary to Read Real Science in Order to Understand Environmental and Safety Policy and Politics

The Environmental Protection Agency sets its standard for regulating chemicals at roughly four hundred thousand times above any known damage to man or beast. Is this what EPA should be doing to protect a vulnerable public? Or is this criterion of choice likely to result in vast expenditures, immense delays, and decline in competitiveness with no health or environmental advantages whatsoever? Would a political scientist's analysis of the policy and politics involved be the same whichever way the researcher answered these questions?

Regulation of low-level exposure to chemicals suspected of causing cancer is largely based on tests involving small animals, usually rats or mice or hamsters or guinea pigs. In order to adjust for the relationship between these very small creatures and much larger human beings and for the huge difference in dose to which each is exposed, it is necessary to rely on statistical models. If there are many available models whose consequences for human health differ from dozens to thousands to tens of thousands of times, without the investigator being able to determine which is the appropriate model, because the mechanism of cancer causation is not understood, does that mean animal tests are the best we can do or that they are utterly useless? If a student asks how to get from Minneapolis to St. Paul and is sent by way of Beijing, is that second best? When a political scientist interested in the political process through which environmental and safety decisions are made answers these questions in the negative, should that matter for the way the episode is analyzed?

In the study of acid rain two different measures of acidity are used, an older one and a somewhat more accurate newer one, though both if used consistently should give reasonable results. Suppose, however, a mistake is made and these measures are used together in such a manner as to greatly increase estimates of the harm to lakes and trees from acid rain. Yet the spread of alarm to the public makes no mention of this fact. Should that omission of fact affect consideration of politics in regard to acid rain? Several times I have asked audiences on their honor to raise hands if they knew that all rain is acid; so far, my results are running from one to three per hundred. Are nonscientists and even scientists outside their areas of specialization doomed forever to ignorance, I ask, or is there a reasonable way with a feasible expenditure of time in which intelligent laymen, which is what all of us are outside of our narrow areas of expertise, can inform ourselves well enough to judge whether decisions are made quite close to or very far from existing scientific knowledge? I think there is.

In the mid-1950s, when I first started studying political science, it was not thought necessary for social scientists to learn much of anything about the substance of issues. Institutions, processes, norms, these were our meat, not parts per trillion or biomagnification or whether ninety-seven types of squirrels constitute one species or many. Information of the kind that using similarities in DNA might greatly reduce the postulated number of species compared to other forms of taxonomy was not then thought either necessary or desirable or even, come to think of it, legitimate.

The growth of government, the perceived importance of political economy, and the eventual increase in interest in public policy, all made understanding the substance of policy, from social security (Is there a trust fund? And what exactly does it have in it, if anything? And can government cash in those pieces of paper to pay off its debts?) to international repudiation of debt (Do repudiators suffer grave retribution, as they used to say in the New York City school exams of my day, always, sometimes, or never?), essential. I think the same is now true of scientific literature about real or alleged harm from technology.

When the Graduate School of Public Policy at Berkeley began in 1969, I did not think it necessary for students to learn science along with the many other things they had to learn. The matter was discussed, as I recall, as part of a general discussion of what one might wish students to learn given unlimited time and resources. But it was soon decided that making our students into pseudoscientists would not be as desirable as trying to have them become competent policy analysts.

Had I believed that it was necessary to acquire a proper scientific education (scientific sophistication, I take it, is equivalent to knowing science), learning something about policy analysis in the two years alloted would indeed have been incompatible with learning much about science. Whether one can learn enough about biology or chemistry or physics or geophysics or genetics, whatever, in one to two years, to use that knowledge as a complement to policy analysis is questionable; it is far easier for this purpose to have a scientifically trained person learn how to be a policy analyst. But it is not, I have come to believe, necessary to face this question because it is possible for laymen without prior preparation to read scientific literatures and make sense of them for policy purposes.

I taught myself how to read science or, better put, I learned whether I could make enough sense out of scientific literatures to be useful, by reading about five subjects over a period of several years—Love Canal, asbestos in schoolrooms, animal tests for suspected carcinogens, the release of genetically engineered organisms into the environment, and global warming. After I thought I knew something about the problems of reading scientific papers, I began a large research project on the relation between knowledge and action in environmental and safety matters. In this project, as well as in regular courses, I ask students to investigate the charges against chemicals like DDT or PCBs or dioxins or to investigate a particular episode, like Times Beach, Missouri, by reading the original scientific literatures.

There are two basic directions that must be followed in order for individuals without scientific background (say members of garden clubs, operators of computer networks, or students at liberal arts colleges) to read articles in scientific journals so as to understand the nature of these controversies and to arrive at their own view. The first rule is one of ego strength—you can do it. Without this belief, novices are easily persuaded that the task is impossible, at least for them. The second, and last, and more directive rule is not to stop when one reads words, phrases, sentences, or paragraphs or even entire papers that one cannot understand. Were this rule not followed, the would-be reader of scientific literatures might not make it past the first or second sentence. Let me put this rule in a more positive way: read only what you do understand and read that slowly and carefully.

Why does the rule of reading only what the reader understands work as well as it does? For one thing, articles in scientific journals are blessedly short. Therefore the lay reader is not dependent on a single article. Rather, the lay reader may hope to learn from twenty to forty articles averaging no more than, say, two or three pages. For another, controversies are in many ways easier to understand than basic science. In controversies, authors desire to make their points and to refute the opposition. If the lay reader perseveres, she will understand what the differences are about and why scientists on the various sides differ. By keeping notes about differences, the point at issue gradually becomes clarified. Often, the reader finds a few review articles whose authors hopefully seek to place the rival arguments next to each other. Thus the lay reader comes to comprehend who differs with whom about what and why.

The wise lay reader understands that he is not a scientist and has no pretense of becoming one. He knows that he is not getting a broad-gauged scientific understanding and, being wise, knows that it would be too time consuming to get one. What a lay reader wants and gets is a pretty good idea of what is generally agreed and what is not. There is almost no disagreement, for instance, that the dangers of something going wrong with the release of genetically engineered organisms into the environment are exceedingly remote. It helps to understand that the parties to the dispute disagree about whether these remote and improbable dangers constitute a threat and not whether they are at all likely to occur.[1] No one reading a variety of pieces about global warming, for instance, would believe those who peddle the line that there is consensus among scientists on this subject. The lay reader would soon discover that scientists do agree that, other things being equal, more CO_2 upstairs means greater warming. But the dispute revolves around whether other factors, like oceans and kelp beds and winds and solar flux, might not alter or even reverse this one effect.[2] Then the claim of consensus can be seen for what it is, a tactic in the struggle over whose views will be accepted and become the basis for public policy.

There are a few things that the interested layman needs to know that can be made available. One is how to use computer search routines to locate this literature. Another is a little instruction in the "cobweb" method of following leads from one footnote to another. Dictionaries of scientific terms and, especially, some idea of nomenclature about relative size and weights, can be most helpful. It is also useful to know what kind of person with what kind of training is most useful to consult about a particular area. In regard to chemicals, for instance, toxicologists are the right people. They exist almost everywhere and, in my experience, are willing to be helpful if the lay analyst has taken the trouble to inform himself about the literature in the field. There is no need to be deterred by the belief that great precision is required. The knowledge, for instance, that trace amounts of something are or are not likely to cause harm to individuals, whereas occupational exposure might well do so, is about as precise as a student of politics and policy needs to get.

Because the very idea is forbidding, a more detailed itinerary for this journey into the scientific heartland is in order. Beginning by undertaking either a computer search or obtaining an index to scientific periodicals in which articles relating to your subject, say Love Canal, or lead, or some class of chemical you never heard of, say, tuolene or PCBs, are found, look for an article containing a review of the literature. If you don't find one, begin with any article. Then follow the footnotes to other articles. This is called, appropriately, the cobweb method.

Begin reading. Circle only those sentences or phrases you can understand, however few. Read these over slowly two to three times. Keep reading and rereading.

By the end of the first five articles you should expect to be thoroughly confused. Go back to rule one: You can (and will) do it. By the tenth article you should know what a few of the disagreements are about but perhaps not yet be cognizant of the big picture. Somewhere around the twentieth article the lay investigator should begin to get the warm and welcome glow of deja vu. There probably are only seventeen to thirty-two (a mythical but cozy number) things to know about a subject and when you know these the rest gets repetitive pretty fast.

Now make lists of arguments pro and con from the various papers. As you read further, consider only the information that bears on these arguments. Stop at the sixth paper that adds no enlightenment.

By this time you know the state of play: what the arguments and the differences are about. Then you can call or write the scientists involved, or scientists nearby (ecologists, toxicologists, biochemists, immunologists, whomever) and ask them questions designed to clarify your remaining doubts. Going back and forth between contending positions and the people who hold them is helpful and, my students have found, fun.

Remember always that you are a citizen and not a scientist. Your task is to use the knowledge you have accumulated to help yourself and your fellow citizens to improve their judgments about what ought and ought not be done (note: this might be read in conjunction with a chapter called "Citizens as Analysts," in an earlier book, *Speaking Truth to Power*, 2nd ed. [New Brunswick, N.J.: Transaction Press, 1986], pp. 252–79). Is the potential danger being discussed substantial and immediate, requiring fast action; is it trivial and overblown, so should be ignored; would a little cleanup and alleviation suffice to protect health or would only a massive effort protect human health or prevent severe environmental degradation? Your reading and discussion will prove sufficient to educate your policy preferences. And that is all a citizen can ask.

The task is formidable, even forbidding, but it is by no means hopeless. As a citizen, moreover, the investigator should have credibility among other citizens. Indeed, if you imagine that your effort is part of a group endeavor in which other people are investigating the other potential risks, the interplay should take on less the aura of advice coming down from on high and more of an exchange of information among individuals who have a lot to contribute to each other's continuing education. When experts disagree, or when the citizen cannot tell whether they disagree, and about what, it is up to us, the lay public, to find out for ourselves.

Understanding what these disputes are about in the sense of locating them within existing knowledge enables lay investigators to ask much better questions. Most things that could be asked have already been asked and given a variety of answers in the scientific literature. Once a person with expertise sees that her questioner has basic understanding, the expert is likely to be much more forthcoming. My students have had excellent results in talking with scientists who write the literature they have read.

If one wishes to see what genuine empowerment looks like, observe a student whose paper shows that she has understood the scientific issues in a controversy and come to a reasoned conclusion. She knows not only that she has mastered something she once believed was way beyond her but, in talking with and reading papers by other students, she also knows that she can learn what she needs to know when she needs to know it should such questions arise in the future.

In various literatures on democracy and science, it is often said that democracy requires a scientifically literate population. Given a grandiose view of what that requires, our collective hearts might well sink. But if democracy requires rather a capacity of intelligent people to discover the information they require and to make sense of it, our hopes may rise. Of course, this attainment comes at a cost in time and effort. For the run of the mill problem, usually involving low level exposure to some chemical, an expenditure of some one hundred to two hundred hours should be sufficient. This is only an effort that can be made every once in a while, an effort that, if exerted in combination with friends, neighbors, or club members, can lead to growing understanding and feelings of confidence. Were a club to do from something like five to eight such issues a year, dividing them among an equivalent number of members, in a five-year period it would have substantial grasp of twenty-five to forty environmental and safety issues. It would be a powerhouse.

As things stand, a stroll down the aisle of the environmental section of a bookstore will be sufficient to persuade anyone of the books' apocalyptic character. Then voices are heard saying the equivalent of "your father's mustache," it isn't so, etc. How is the poor citizen to tell the difference? Our society is so polarized over these issues that we may actually have to rely on widespread citizen understanding. What is regarded as the least likely alternative, namely, widespread citizen understanding and participation, appears to me the only hope of narrowing the gap between knowledge and action in environmental and safety episodes. If that is so, the standards for understanding these matters must now include first-hand acquaintance with the original research reports around which these controversies continue to swirl. Experience persuades me that by following simple rules individuals of ordinary intelligence can learn what they need to know by reading original scientific literatures rather than books devoted to reassurance or to alarm. By preparing themselves to interrogate experts, indeed, by going between experts with rival views, it is possible to sharpen understanding of why there are disagreements. And by talking to friends, neighbors, and workmates it is possible for citizens to develop their own preferences.

Once-upon-a-time, it was thought necessary to protect democracy against the machinations of the Dr. Strangeloves of this world who would hide their moral obtuseness or viciousness behind a command of exotic lore. Now all sides have their scientists. The battle is not even but neither is it lopsided. It is even enough to change the problem from hidden manipulation to how to choose between rival views based on access to the same exoticlore. The scientific lore is more exotic than ever but the controveries give us-the-people a better chance to make up our own minds.

Notes

1. See Aaron Wildavsky, "Public Policy," in Bernard D. Davis, ed., *The Genetic Revolution* (Baltimore: Johns Hopkins University Press, 1991), pp. 77–104.
2. See Aaron Wildavsky, "Global Warming As a Means of Achieving an Egalitarian Society: A Foreword" to *The Heated Debate by Robert Balling (San Francisco: Pacific Research Institute, forthcoming).*

10

Review of *Acts of Meaning* by Jerome Brunner

Just as universalism triumphs in science, economics, and war, movements in the social sciences and humanities seek to replace universalistic with particularistic standards. Instead of prediction, which narrows the circle of winners to a favored few, there is interpretation in which many can not only be called but also chosen as each is as valid as the other. Instead of theories subject to disconfirmation, there are narratives whose criteria of excellence are internal, that is, suitable to the particular people involved, and not external, subject to standards applicable to everyone. When one realizes that democracy has been justified on the basis of citizens' ability to choose among publically accessible arguments, the questions raised by various movements calling themselves deconstruction or interpretation or, here, cultural psychology, become less esoteric.

My own view is that the social sciences and their applied subfields, like policy analysis, should take account of the construction of meanings and that this awareness requires greater attention to the subjective element in human life. It is not only that individuals may have different preferences but that they perceive problems differently that matters. Who else could confer meaning if not human beings? That does not mean, however, that subjectivity cannot be studied in a more or less objective (I should say "inter-subjective") manner. The crucial difference lies between those who wish to alter not only the theoretical perspectives through which society is studied but also to change the rules of the game about what constitutes evidence. I prefer to alter the theories but to keep the rules.

To those accustomed to looking for the political morals and the intellectual messages of the times among the entrails of academic theories, it comes as no surprise that those who wish to live lives of graded distinction (call them hierarchists) as well as those who wish to live lives of external competition (individualists) are appalled at the rise of rampant subjectivism while those who believe in diminishing power distinctions among people ("egalitarians" seems like a fair designation) welcome the change. Doubt it? Show me a deconstructionist who is conservative or an interpretivist who isn't liberal.

I have put my key to this theoretical roman à clef up front in order to counter the common view that all this fuss about meaning is meaningless. On the contrary, the controversy over interpretism is about the most meaningful question of all—how people should live with each other.

In the same spirit, Jerome Brunner's *Acts of Meaning* is about how he would redirect his home field of psychology away from biological determinism, away from the human mind as an information processer, away from stimulus and response models with their "little studies" of overtly observable behavior, and toward the social construction of meaning. His short book, he tells his readers, is written

> to illustrate what a psychology looks like when it concerns itself centrally with meaning, how it inevitably becomes a cultural psychology and how it must venture beyond the conventional aims of positivist science with its ideals of *reductionism, causal explanation* and *prediction*. The three need not be treated like the Trinity. For when we deal with meaning and culture, we inevitably move toward another ideal. . . . [T]o insist upon explanation in terms of "causes" simply bars us from trying to understand how human beings interpret their worlds and how *we* interpret *their* acts of interpretation. And if we take the object of psychology (as of any intellectual enterprise) to be the achievement of understanding, why is it necessary under all conditions for us to understand in *advance* of the phenomena to be observed—which is all that prediction is? Are not plausible interpretations preferable to causal explanations, particularly when the achievement of a causal explanation forces us to artificialize what we are studying to a point almost beyond recognition as representative of human life?

Without going into how plausibility is determined, Brunner's Trinity is synonymous with the craft rules of the scientific enterprise.

Put one way, as the formulation of hypotheses about how people make sense out of their world, Brunner's cultural psychology is no different from any other kind of theorizing. If meanings are negotiated, as I agree they are, then there would seem to be no barrier to forming generalizations about these negotiations. Why, then, abandon the test of predictability? If we can't say what sort of people with what type of commitment for living with others engage in what kind of negotiations with what sort of likely results, then all we are doing is beating our gums.

Actually, Brunner denies that he is making psychology more subjective; on the contrary, he claims that "by virtue of participation in culture, meaning is rendered *public* and *shared*." It is not enough to prefer one's own meaning, I agree, for one must also convince others to share it. Why, then, get rid of the concept of causality? Brunner disputes "Our preoccupation with verification as criteria of meaning." It is one thing, of course, to say that what we cannot verify is nonsense and quite another to say that science ought to aim at verification (or, more precisely, propositions that are refutable). Why, then, should I take Jerome Brunner's word in preference to that of anyone else whose propositions cannot be refuted?

The distrust of subjectivism, Brunner thinks, may be due to people's erroneous impressions of the gap between what individuals say and what they do. To Brunner, however, what people say is as important as what they do.[1] There is, to be sure, everything to be said in favor of studying the relationship between saying and doing. So let's do it. If, as folk wisdom has it, there is no connection between the two, the theorist would have to explain how it is possible for people to stay together without being able to justify to each other their way of living together. If there are constraints on using other cultures' rhetoric (egalitarians do not refer to nature as cornucopian because they would then have difficulty in justifying sharing out, and individualists do not describe nature as fragile because that would make it hard to resist regulation), as I believe, then these should be specified and compared with what has, is, and will happen. Suspicious? Observe how environmental versus libertarian groups refer to nature as they appeal for funds; evidence is as close as your mailbox.

My comments come from within a social constructivist perspective. Therefore I agree when Brunner says "I believe that we shall be able to interpret meanings and meaning-making in a principled manner only in the degree to which we are able to specify the structure and coherence of the larger contexts in which speech meanings are created and transmitted." But what are these contexts? Brunner says a lot about language. But language is for everyone; it cannot explain the conflicts over meaning that Brunner keeps saying he wants to study. Essentially, Brunner asks how social stability is created in the midst of different constructions of reality. He answers that each society must have "interpretative procedures for adjudicating the different construels of reality that are inevitable in any diverse society." This is thin gruel. True, as he says, we witness a " 'battle of lifestyles.' " But how can that be? For Brunner talks entirely as if there were a single culture in each society. How, then, if reality is deemed a social construct, find any other source of reality out there? If the source of preferences lies in society, in our social relations, as Brunner stipulates earlier, then the source of divergence must lie in the different ways of life that constitute the given society. Without cultural pluralism, in short, all the talk about putting meaning back into social science is empty.

The "self as a storyteller" is one of Brunner's major themes. Brunner tells us that these include "some that are feared and some hoped for, all crowding to take possession of a Now Self." But how many Possible

Selves, as Markus and Nurius call them, can there be? If the number of possible selves is infinite, there is no point in going further because there would no prospect of a social science, each self being different from others. The postulation of an infinite number of selves would also call into question the possibility of human communication and therefore of society. If there are only a few such selves, what are they, how are they formed, what makes them viable, how do they communicate, can they be extinguished? Why hasn't the best self, proved by experience, driven out the other contenders? There is no sense in asking any such questions without doing what a social theory requires, namely, reducing the variety of human life through theoretical constructs. No reductionism, no theory, no prediction, no retrodiction (history), no explanation. Only tall tales.

Without stipulating who the cultural players are, what each is trying to achieve (that is, their vision of how people should live), there appears to be a lot shouting without substance. And that explains, I think, why this whole interpretative turn has proved so puzzling. Interpretivism is shrouded in the unwillingness of those who claim to impart meaning to human life to take a stand on what way of life has most meaning for them. Deconstruction and interpretation for what is the question.

Applying principles of social construction to these modes of knowing, those who deny authority to texts or authors, who see hidden, hierarchical power behind every pretext, who will take no stand except to say that no stand makes sense, wish to diminish social as they do literary or economic or political distinctions. This has a name: it is egalitarianism. But then it too would be partial, a "special interest," blatantly political. So the more radical posture of undermining the authority of language is taken.

A distinguished psychologist, Brunner wants to share his newfound understanding with the rest of us. By portraying the struggle as one between those with rather desiccated and overly formal, narrow and restricted views of social science, and those with more expansive and more warmly embracing views of life in social and historical context, rather than between rival cultures, Brunner slights the possibility of joining new concepts to the oldtime scientific religion to the benefit of both.

Notes

1. He claims, erroneously, in my opinion, that there are few studies illuminating "how what one does reveals what one thinks or feels or believes." This is exactly the subject matter that in economics is called revealed preference. Indeed, a discipline that does not want to admit the formation of preferences into its house, finds revealed preference useful because it enables scholars to estimate what people believe from what they do. I am dubious but that is a theme for another occasion.

11

Has Modernity Killed Objectivity?

Science does not require that observers exhibit the pristine purity of total detachment. No one, save perhaps a tyro, suggests that a scientist be so chaste, or that "scientific habits of mind" are incompatible with "passionate advocacy, strong faith, intuitive conjecture, and imaginative speculation." All of us, scientists included, are subject to countless influences so well hidden as to be uncoverable either by socio- or psychoanalysis. To transform a scientist into that fully aseptic and thoroughly neutral observer of legend is a virtual impossibility. There is no doubt that "there is more to seeing than meets the eyeball"; that what we see is "theory-laden" or "field-determined." We can admit out of hand that there is no such process as "immaculate perception." Arguments, therefore, which seek to sustain objectivity by predicating neutrality are doomed to fail. They are also irrelevant. Even if such neutral observers could be manufactured, Popper tells us, "they could not possibly attain to what we call scientific objectivity."

For the crux of this concept rests on the fact that men, even scientific men, are not angels. Indeed, the entire system of science is based on a variation of Murphy's Law—the prime assumption that any scientist, no matter how careful he may be, is a risky actor; that he is prone to error; that he is not perfectable; that there are no algorithms which he can apply so perfectly as to expunge any and all biasing effects. Accordingly, all his proposals must be subject to error-correcting procedures. The goals of the enterprise demand a network of highly redundant and visible public checks to protect against the inclusion of erroneous items in the corpus of knowledge. Such networks are institutionalized control procedures *which continually subject "all scientific statements to the test of independent and impartial criteria": not men, but criteria, for science recog-*

nizes "no authority of persons in the realm of
cognition." This is the decision rule that is called
objectivity.

—Martin Landau

The debate over multiculturalism is rooted in two major conflicts over values, the more obvious being the difference between equal opportunity and equality of result, and the less obvious, which I shall pursue here, between modernity and objectivity. The suggestion that education should be multicultural contains the scarcely veiled supposition that race, gender, and (sometimes) sexual orientation matter more than knowledge. Objections arise on the grounds that the use of ascriptive criteria in selection of teachers would lead to a decrease in knowledge. Of course, if universities merely privilege the appearance of knowledge by calling it "objective," when there is no such thing, then it is no great loss or may even be a gain to de-privilege this false objectivity. Thus multiculturalism is linked to interpretivism and deconstruction in that they all require an end to claims of objective knowledge.

Has objectivity become passé? Has the increased sophistication brought by modern understandings revealed objectivity to be a "noble lie," useful in driving mankind to its first scientific understandings but revealed by domination? Are the social sciences especially blameworthy in failing to acknowledge the biases revealed by the social study of the social sciences as struggles for power rather than for knowledge?

Subjectivity already has considerable standing in social science. It is widely acknowledged that individuals do not necessarily make decisions on the basis of the way the world is, but rather on the way they perceive it to be, a subjective state if there ever was one. It is further agreed that all perception is selective; no one sees it all or can get it all; the human mind is not a swivel operating at the speed of light that can see in all directions seemingly simultaneously. Rather, the opportunity cost, as an economist might say, of what is selected in is all the rest that is selected out of a particular vision. Indeed, it is said to be a singular virtue of scientific theories that they leave out so much in order to make what is included narrower in range but more powerful in prediction. All sorts of biases, moreover, whether material or ideological or based on class or gender or race or region—the list is as long as our considerable capacities for distortion—influence our perceptions. Given all this and more, where is the place for objectivity? Put this way, is not the amazing thing that anybody ever believed in objectivity?

It is one thing to say, following the religious, that we see through a glass darkly, of necessity, and quite another to say that there is no underlying truth or reality there to be perceived. A belief in the importance of subjectivity does not necessarily negate the existence of objectivity, that is, the effort to come to a closer, better, less subjective understanding. Subjectivity, in short, has its limits and these need to be understood.

It is important to demonstrate that different people in different social contexts who adhere to different ways of life often perceive the same or similar objects or behaviors or situations markedly differently. Nowadays, for instance, we witness estimates of danger from technology that vary thousands of times over, not merely by a few percent here or there. That is bedrock; we observe these differences as sure as anything. And they do call out for explanation. But differences in perception, however deep they run, are not the same as differences in manipulative ability. Stating your subjective opinion or even explaining the subjectivity of yourself and others is not equivalent to making the world and the people in it do what you want or turn out the way you wish. To claim that the human mind can transport itself and the body in which it is encased to distant planets is one thing; getting there is something else again. Only by being in touch with the way the world really is, at least in part, can such transport be made. Communists and their supporters praised the Soviet-style command economy for decades, to take another example, but they could not make it work.

The natural sciences proceed in significant part by way of "impossibility theories" devoted to stating what cannot happen according to known principles. Social science ought to do more of that. If we did, the feeling of theoretical déjà vu, nothing is ever refuted, every fool notion comes back, would not be ever present. In the 1920s and 1930s Ludwig von Mises and Friedrich von Hayek, adherents of the subjectivist Austrian school of economics, which they helped create, argued negatively that no economy based on central command principles could succeed in growing over time and positively that only economies based on spontaneous interactions as found in markets could grow over time. For decades their ideas were largely rejected because command economies did grow. So far as we know now, Mises and Hayek have been proven correct, though, as is only proper, all theories are conditional in the sense that they may be overtaken by still better ones.

The integrity of science, as Michael Polanyi noted in his seminal essay, "The Republic of Science," does not depend on the integrity of individual scientists but on a competitive system that separates the best from the worst independent of any single person's will. By insisting that no one's authority is final, and by demanding the replication of experiments, far-flung and dispersed communities of scientists are able to do better for science than anyone can do alone. Polanyi did not say, no doubt because he could not imagine anyone would contest the point, that science would do better if scientists sought truer conceptions of the way the world works rather than seeking falsehood. Were there no truth to be discovered, science might proceed on the basis of seeking untruths without harm. Indeed, it is difficult to imagine how scientists would keep a straight face with one another or even bother to do their daily craft work if their assumption was that there was no truer reality to be discovered. Of course, even if they were on track as judged by their peers and by the use of their ideas in practical work, it is always possible, indeed likely, that there are deeper conceptions of the underlying reality that will one day take the place of existing theories. But the absence of a final truth does not mean there is none at all.

Conceiving of science as competition over ideas, science is also about conflict and therefore about power. Recall Robert K. Merton's law to the effect that, in any biography or autobiography of a scientist, after it is first stated that he cared not for precedence, it would take no more than twenty pages to find him engaged in a battle royal over that very thing. Fame is a spur. Over time, however, we know of few scientific ideas accepted against increasingly negative evidence. For as long as there exist diverse groups of independent scientists, there is no way to control them all.

Against this view of the progressive improvement of scientific theories, there is the contention that science is inevitably politicized and that to contend otherwise is sheer rubbish. On the contrary, I claim, it is the view of inevitable politicization that reflects trashy thought. It is equivalent to the famous old joke about the child who kills his parents and then claims the mercy of the court because he has become an orphan. As Martin Landau teaches,

> all classifications, no matter how natural they appear, are invented. They are constructs which permit us to take a *first glance,* to engage in a search to make observations. If we permit them to congeal, if we reify them, if we fail to make the necessary distinction between class and object, between category and assignment, then we rob ourselves of the opportunity to take a second glance (research). One needs to emphasize that category-informed observation takes the form of a search and that the concept of a re-search constitutes an error-correcting device.[1]

For nothing in and of itself or by itself is either politicized or unpoliticized. The quality of being political is not something natural in the world, as if it could be plucked like a fruit from a tree, but is rather something imposed, a social rather than a natural construction of knowledge. Everything that governments do, for instance, whether this be warfare or imprisonment, has been done sometimes, somewhere privately and whatever has been done privately, including raising children, has been done publicly. In short, what should be private or public, political or nonpolitical, is what we contest about. When disagreements are large and deep among political activists, as is now true in the United States, then one side makes greater efforts to politicize and the other to resist politicization. Ground more finely, parties and factions may want to politicize this (say, decisions about hiring faculty) and depoliticize that (same-gender sex). Which is not to say that one cannot legitimately argue about the consequences of politicizing family life or sports or social science. The record does not speak kindly of such efforts, from Lysenkoism in the Soviet Union to experiments on live human beings claiming erroneously to prove racial superiority by the Nazis. But "the political," as some loosely call it, is not a fixed quality or quantity, known independently of our will, but a product of social interaction to gain agreement.

The right question to ask is not "What is political?" but rather "What do we want to make political?" In the humanities, especially in literature, the urge to combine subjectivism with politicization has reached new heights under the name of "deconstruction." At one level, deconstruction is a literary critical art that has been practiced for a long time. Virtually everyone, I think, agrees that rich and varied texts, like Bibles and Greek tragedies, are subject to more than one interpretation in that good arguments can be put foward in behalf of each perspective. On this basis, however, few would have been interested in pursuing deconstruction further. It is radical deconstruction, the denial that texts have meaning or that authors can control them, the straightforward avowal that the purpose of literary criticism is to be, as they put it, perennially subversive, that has converted deconstruction from a fad into a movement. Yet, if all there is to literary criticism is already in the critic, there is good reason to ask why the exercise for which he is paid is necessary.

Let us ask a simple question: Can you think of a single deconstructionist who is a political conservative? There may be a very few but the predonderant proportion must be liberal-cum-political radicals. What is the essence of this radicalism? It is a belief in greater equality of condition as a desirable norm for regulating social interacation. From this norm of radical egalitarianism comes immense hostility to existing authority as redolent of oppressive hierarchies and inegalitarian markets. Applied to literature, radical egalitarianism requires radical deconstruction, that is, an unceasing attack on authority, in this case the authority of words, sentences, paragraphs, and entire texts, as incoherent, indeed, as meaning exactly the opposite of whatever it appears to mean. The advantage is that literary critics can pursue a radical egalitarian agenda without joining a party or overtly adhering to any ideology other than what appears to be nihilism but is actually radical egalitarianism. The disadvantage, as John Ellis demonstrates in *Against Deconstruction,* is incoherence.

The subject of subjectivity, as we have seen, is something of a sport for intellectuals. It is, however, a game with deadly purpose, namely, the delegitimation of authority in democracies on the grounds that these are mere covers for unconscionable inequalities, the worse in that the ideologues of democracy profess exactly the opposite. Combatting such constant criticism is not an easy task in a democracy that prides itself on being open to different viewpoints and which cannot, therefore, cut down on discourse without violating its fundamental principles. Democracy is based on a belief that its people are able to make reasoned judgments between opposing viewpoints. When scientific issues become impossible for the public to understand, because those who speak as scientists do not even agree on how to frame the questions, an important part of democracy in action is lost. Worse, when "noble lies" are told in the belief that the system is so bad any argument against it can only counteract a small part of its falsehoods, the task of the citizen is made much more difficult. As the German communists used to say, nach Hitler uns (after Hitler us), only something infinitely worse came after they had helped delegitimate the Weimar government.

"Multiculturalism," as it is called today, is a misnomer. To the people who purvey it, variety means uniformity. Using a term, "multi," which implies that ordinary social science and humanities teach only one way of life while the proponents of multiculturalism teach a number of different ways, when their purpose is to inculcate a single way, takes some doing.

It runs counter to knowledge to claim that race or gender or class represent forms of "culturalism" in that people of the same race, class, or gender live the same way of life. In my courses on political cultures I show that among American Indian and Black African peoples can be found hierarchical, individualist, and egalitarian cultures, as anthropologists have known for a very long time. When a single culture, egalitarianism, is imposed in the name of cultural pluralism, discourse has been debased.

Subjectivism is a necessary aspect of science, social science, and the humanities; it is also a snare if it becomes a substitute for seeking truth. Hypotheses may be proposed in all our subjectivity, but testing and tentative acceptance, followed by retesting, requires institutions that are plural, independent, and competitive but whose members share criteria requiring continuous resort to evidence. The proper use of subjectivity, in sum, depends on widespread commitment to objectivity.

Notes

1. Martin Landau, *Political Theory and Political Science* (New York: Macmillan, 1972), p. 50.

Index

Advance Reviews

"With lithe, clear prose and a deep sense of place, Mark Hannon's *The Vultures* is a novel that balances those elusive qualities that any reader craves: a page-turner that still nourishes a literary heartbeat; a story about unique characters but also about the soul of a city; social commentary and political intrigue relevant to any period. Vietnam-era Buffalo comes to life in these pages, reminiscent of Dennis Lehane on Boston or Richard Russo on Rust-Belt America."

> — Brad Felver, author of the short story collection
> *The Dogs of Detroit*

"If Charles Willeford and his noir notebook had shadowed the denizens of the Queen City on Erie, this is the book he would have written. Before Hannon forged the prose, he made his bones the old-school way in Buffalo. As Sartre said, 'It disturbs me no more to find men base, unjust or selfish than to see . . . vultures ravenous ...'"

> — Rafael Alvarez, author of *Orlo and Leini Meet the Invisible Man*

"*The Vultures* is a thrilling multilayered story set in the seventies, featuring detective Pat Brogan, an equally complex and believable protagonist. Hannon does a wonderful job pulling it all together so that it is utterly readable."

> — David Swinson, author of *Trigger* and *The Second Girl*